"Words can make a tremendous difference in how
you say things."

Shelley Stockwell

"We, your guiding angels serve and love you. Drop
your veil of fear and let our words move upon your
page. You overflow beauty, guidance and love."

Archangel Michael
as written through Shelley

This book teaches me to write automatically;
from simple phrase to painting dramatically.
What it is. How it's done.
I expand my awareness while having fun!

also by Shelley Lessin Stockwell

Books
- **Insides Out**
- **Sex and Other Touchy Subjects**
- **Time Travel: Do-It-Yourself Past Life Journey Handbook**
- **Self Hypnosis: Smile on Your Face, Money in Your Pocket**
- **Denial Is Not A River In Egypt:**
  Unveil Denial, Depression & Addiction and Feel Terrific!

Audio Cassettes
- **Time Travel Journey**
- **Mer-Ka-Ba: Ascension To The 4th Dimension**
- **Automatic Writing**
- **Yes I Can!**
- **Peace and Calm**
- **Sleep, Beautiful Sleep**
- **Lose Weight!**
- **Yes, You Can Quit Smoking**
- **No More Alcohol**
- **No More Sugar Junkie**
- **Overcome Depression, Addiction & Compulsion**
- **The Wellness Tape**
- **Great Golf**
- **The Money Tape**

Video
- **Trance-Formations: Hypnosis, Channeling & Past Life Regressions**

Music & Song
- **Sex and Other Touchy Subjects**

Audio Cassettes For Kids
- **Mommy Bunny's Going to Work**
- **Your Are What You Eat & The Dinosaur Rap**

These and others available from Creativity Unlimited Press.
See order forms at the end of this book.

Automatic Writing & Hieroscripting

Tap Unlimited Creativity & Guidance

By Shelley Lessin Stockwell

 CREATIVITY UNLIMITED PRESS™

CREATIVITY UNLIMITED LEARNING INSTITUTE
♡ CREATIVITY UNLIMITED PRESS™
30819 CASILINA
RANCHO PALOS VERDES, CA. 90275
(310) 541-4844

ISBN #0-912559-25-X
LIBRARY OF CONGRESS NUMBER 91-90382

PRINTED IN THE USA

ACKNOWLEDGEMENTS

My love and gratitude to the beautiful angel, Jessica Kaitlin Morris and her mother Diane and her father Jeff: you made this book possible.

Special thanks also to Beryl Middleton, Sandy Medearis, Judy Walker, Ewa Carlsson, Don Bay, Barbara McNurlin, Jon Nicholas, Corinne Hartley, Lynn Morgan, Bryce Stockwell and all my devoted friends, students and readers. Thanks too to Scott Corbern, and all the other producers, directors and hosts of the *Phil Donahue Show* and *The Other Side*. Each of you offered the support and encouragement that made and makes a big difference.

And of course, my love to my awesome guides; Kendra, Red Feather, Isis, Archangel Michael and the dozens of others who bring me wisdom. I am full of de•light!

FOREWORD

By Ormond McGill

I have been asked to write the foreword to this book. It is a HOW TO book about automatic writing and hieroscripting. Automatic writing is writing spontaneously via the subconscious mind rather than through conscious mind deliberate writing. You could call it "subjective writing," if you wish.

Hieroscripting is like automatic writing and is subjective, but instead of writing what comes forth is in the nature of symbolic drawing. Automatic writing is wonderful and belongs to the domain of the poet. Hieroscripting is wonderful and belongs to the domain of the artist. And there is a dimension of sound sometimes added to it too, which belongs to the domain of the musician.

I could say that Shelley Lessin Stockwell's book about automatic writing and hieroscripting is an instructional manual to perform these subject skills, but that would do an injustice to the full value of the book, as she not only shows you HOW TO, she takes you deep into the transcendental and the spiritual in the learning. And she handles it all with a touch of humor. Good thing, otherwise it might scare you to death, and that would promote a lie for the truth you will find herein is that there is no death at all. There is only a continuum of life.

Death becomes recognized as but a transitional stage from life in form to life in the formless, followed by a returning to the form. Over an over again, Immortality.

Reincarnation?

Whether or not you believe in reincarnation is irrelevant. It is the way of the universe: a star exists for eons of time, but it finally dies and becomes a "black hole" in space, providing an opportunity to renew its energies. More eons pass and it is reborn anew. That is the pattern. And you follow that pattern too, as you are a miniature of the universe. Every moment something within you dies and is reborn anew. Yourself is the living proof.

And in that space between death and birth lies the realm of spirit. This book instructs the reader in how to contact the realm of spirit. And what a joy it is to know that loved ones are never lost.

And for the scientific minded, here are detailed instructions for the cultivating of both gifts of automatic writing and hieroscripting with which one can objectively experiment.

Test it for yourself and see how truly wonderful you really are. You are a miracle, you know.

Dr. Ormond McGill
Dean of American Hypnosis

photo by Jon Nicholas

Shelley Lessin Stockwell

INTRODUCTION

Dearest Reader,

Life's surprising twists and turns mold and form us. Through an amazing set of circumstances my life took a giant one/eighty. The result you hold in your hand at this moment. I believe that the simple techniques in this book will put a new spin to your life too.

In 1981, I didn't know what automatic writing was and I thought that a channel was something you swim in England. I was working as both a hypnotherapist and a flight attendant with TWA at that time. While on a layover in Dayton, Ohio I was jolted awake by a beam of light shining through the window onto my face. In the loud voice it said "Shelley". The light *spoke* in the voice of my deceased father, Irv.

I thought: "This is crazy. The light talked, I know it was my father's voice but he's dead. I know I'm not dreaming. This really happened."

I was afraid to tell anyone. It seemed so strange. Weeks later, in a magazine article about near-death experiences, I read that people who die and come back often have encounters with white light and deceased loved ones. Perhaps, I had a near death experience I reasoned.

Around that time I befriended a flight attendant named Ewa (pronounced Eva) Carlsson. Immediately, I thought of Ewa as a soul-mate friend. One night at Ewa's house a friend, who was studying psychic phenomenon at UCLA, suggested that we try the Ouija board. I'd tried it once before and all it spelled was "k.w.", "k.w." which made no sense to me.

This time, the board wrote:
"I am your father. I live in Ewa."
"What is your message for me?" I asked
The board answered: "Love Pa....Keep Wonder." ("*k. w.!*")

I've always believed that TWA flight attendants were special. <u>T</u>ravel <u>W</u>ith the <u>A</u>ngels (TWA) is true for them. One of these flight attendants was Diane Grimburg Morris. Since I write poetry books, Diane asked me if I would write a birth announcement poem for her expected baby, Jessica Katlin Morris. I did.

I never met little Jessica until four years later, when in June of 1989, Diane called and said: "Jessica is deathly ill. I know that you are a healer. Would you please go to the hospital and heal her?"

I thought of myself as a Hypnotherapist, not a healer, but agreed to go hoping maybe I could assist little Jessica. In a hospital in Laguna Beach, California, I saw a beautiful angelic Jessica hooked up to a breathing apparatus. There was another machine going "beep...beep...beep". Little Jessica showed no response.

I sat with her for two nights and fell in love as I tried desperately to hypnotize her back to health: "Your heart is beating...your lungs are inflating...you feel life surging through you."

Before I left my house the third evening, Ewa called: "Shelley, when you visit Jessica tonight be sure to tell her that if she goes or stays it's between her and God." I promised I would.

I arrived to the saddest birthday party I've ever seen; Barbie Dolls placed lovingly on the chest of a beautiful still little girl. "Happy Birthday Jessica. You're four years old."

After Diana and Jeff (Jessica's mother and father) left the room, I leaned over and said: "Jessica this is your friend Shelley. For the last few nights I've been asking you to live. Tonight I want to say something else. If you live that will be great...but if you go your mother, father and brother will be just fine. If you go, or stay, that's between you and God."

Every buzzer and beeper went off on the machines. The lights blinked and dozens of nurses and doctors raced in. I felt very strange and slithered out of the room. I said to myself: "I shouldn't have done that...I don't know what I'm doing. I don't know what I'm messing with. I feel really strange."

Hours later, Jessica died. I didn't tell Diane and Jeff what had happened with me that night, they were in too much pain. I wrote and delivered Jessica's eulogy. My heart felt broken.

A few weeks later Diane called to tell me that she had visited a trance channel. "A lady who closes her eyes and talks from spirit." Diane said that now she knew Jessica was not gone. Diane called again: She had been sitting alone at the table crying in the middle of the night when she heard a voice in her head say: "Pick up the pencil and put it on the paper."

The pencil wrote the words in scrawly childish hand: "Mommy I love you." "Shelley, Jessica is writing through me. I'm automatic writing my daughter."

Shortly after that, I tried automatic writing poetry and it worked! I taught my creative writing students how to do it too. It was easy to teach and to learn. Because I was completing my 3rd book TIME TRAVEL: The Do-It-Yourself Past Life Journey Handbook, I devised a technique to automatic write past lives.

A year later, Diane got pregnant again and the flight attendants gave her a baby shower. After the shower, I was flabbergasted to received the following thank you note:

Dear Shelley,
I write these words thru my Mommy. I just want to tell you that you were the one who helped me to see the angels and it made my transition to this world most loving and easy. I send you much love and light from this side. You are the one to light the way for many many people. I'll be here for you when it is your time to cross. Avid spirit. Be in the light be in the light Love, Jessica

Six months later, Diane called. By now, when Diane talked I listened. "Shelley I'm going to the Whole Life Expo to see a trance channel will you join me?"

I had never been to a Whole Life Expo and had never seen a trance channel. At the Expo I had an aura photo taken and the psychic who interpreted the photo said: "That white blob above your head is your guardian angel." Next, an astrologer said "The strongest thing in your chart is your guardian angel."

The next day I said to my secretary:
"I can channel."
And she said:
"Do it."

So I closed my eyes, said a little prayer, chanted an "ohm" (like the lady I'd had seen at the Expo) and a voice came through me:

"I am your guardian angel. It is as if my speaking is a rusty door now open. I loosen the rusty door of sound. I will speak more freely. Rust, rust, the snow of time. I speak the tongue of spirit. I was called here now. You called me. Shelley called me to speak as if you had opened a door to a room long closed; rusty and full of memories. The door must learn to swing free and let in the air and sunshine. The door to the room of sleep must open gently. To awaken from the room of sleep when not ready can be hurtful. When the door is open, show respect for the room of awakeness.

She will speak from the heart and confidence will grow. We have chosen her to speak for us. We have chosen many but she is good. She is eccentric. We chose her when she was small. She did not know it. She still does not believe it. She was chosen to speak for us. She must light others so they can wake up. She must stay awake so she can light others. Do not play games, the spirit is to be respected."

The next day while speaking to a psychology class at the local high school about how to use self-hypnosis for self love. I said to the teacher: "I can channel."

"Come back next Monday and channel for my speech class the teacher said."

Monday morning, I channeled for 40 high school students. The messages, especially about the past were so accurate and profound the classroom was stunned. One girl went to a pay phone and called her parents. They in turn asked me to come and channel for them.

Their home and workplace (They own a chain of movie theaters.) had been robbed. Kendra, the channeled spirit that now speaks through me regularly, told the family the name and car license of the robbers.

"The kids at the theater were having a beer party night of the robbery. A boy named Dave's hands got lucky. He opened the safe. Dave is 19 years old and went to Redondo High School"

A skeptical theater owner called the manager of his theater and asked if they were drinking the night of the robbery.

"Yes, we were I was afraid to tell you. We had a beer party."
"Was a guy named Dave there?"
"Yes. But I didn't know him!"

Many phone calls later everyone agreed that a guy named Dave was there. And each thought someone else knew him.

Today I no longer fly for TWA but I still "travel with angels"- lots of them. I speak at Expos all over the United States, not just about the mainstream uses of hypnosis, but, how to automatic write, channel, develop psychic abilities, and heal yourself and others.

My spirits teach others to channel in my playshop "Channeling: You Conduit !:" When we tap our higher self and our guidance, we become into-great-ed in our body mind and now, spirit. My guides say that we are all psychic.

I and my guides were invited to the Great Channeling Conference in Giza, Egypt below the great Pyramid. I and 14 other world famous channels (including Kevin Ryerson, who channeled for Shirley Mc Laine , Barbara Marciniak, author of *Bringers of the Dawn*, and Darryl Anka,'Bashar', Shawn Randall, Andrew Bayuk.), spoke individually and in "panels of channels"

I have since spoken in Japan, Australia and New Zealand and returned to Egypt two more times. I train and certify others in Hypnosis, Transpersonal Hypnotherapy and Past Life Regression in Rancho Palos Verdes, California. We hope to become a fully accredited **University of Creativity and Enlightenment**. Our curriculum to include automatic drawing, painting and writing, hypnosis, sacred geometry, healing and spirituality. Kendra, Isis, Red Feather, Archangel Michael and my other guides say that they will be on the faculty.

So read on and please drop me a note to share with me your amazing experiences.

photo by Sarah Layton

My love to you,

Shelley Lessin Stockwell

P.S. I woke up from a nights sleep and automatic wrote the following message regarding the introductory remarks you just read:

"Most interestingly, she has forgotten the time of opening. She was at camp (15 years she was) and it was to be a moment of recognition. She sat upon a mountain in quiet and we spoke. We told her of the seven basic human needs and commanded that she scribe our words.

She cried as she wrote. She felt our presence and she pushed her golden cord through her neck to the core of her mind. But she was not ready. Her business with her earth family was incomplete. She thought our words to intermesh with her need for recognition; so, when she put the paper down we took it back.

She looked and looked; distressed at the loss. She could not remember what her hand had writ. Now she is ready again. Her essence a fuller vibration. We send blessings and love,

Archangel Michael"

I asked Archangel Michael to automatic write these elusive seven human needs I thought I had "lost" 35 years ago and he did. they are included in the section on communicating with your guides. (page 37.)

TABLE OF CONTENTS

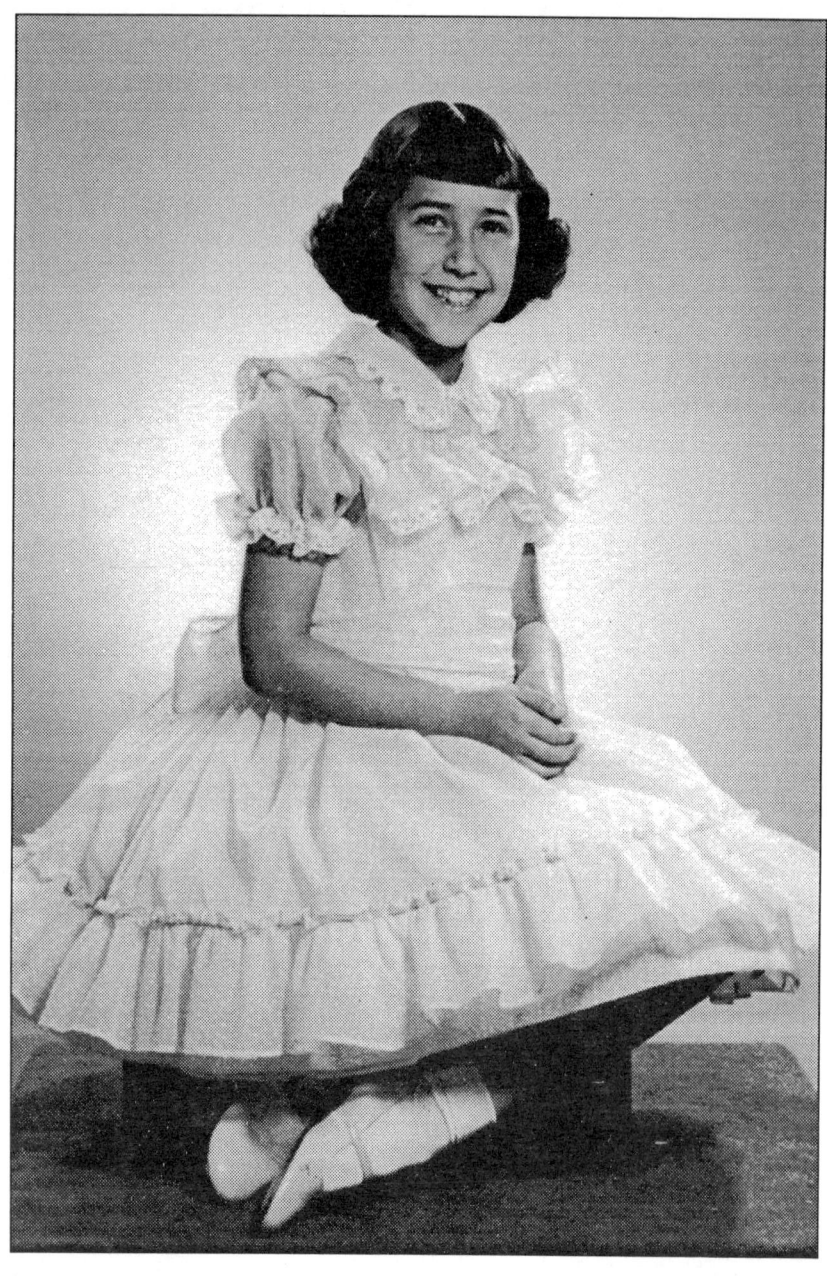

CHAPTER I:

Automatic Writing & Hiero-Scripting

Who in the world is in here now?
For heavens sake and holy cow.
This profound communication
Brings me to Illumination!

A Hieroscripted Drawing by Shelley Lessin Stockwell

AN ANCIENT AND MODERN ART

"All good poets compose their beautiful poems not by art but because they are inspired and possessed."
– Plato

Automatic communication, writing and hiero-scripting has been used since the beginning of recorded history. The ancient Chinese used a planchette; a Ouija board like contraption with a writing implement attached. In the 5th Century B.C. the Greek mathematician Pythagarus used the wheeled Mystic Table. The table rolled over a stone slab that was etched with ancient symbols.

In the 19th Century, a pencil mounted on castors and placed in a wooden wafer was used to write continuous words upon the page. From this contraption evolved our modern Ouija board. During World War I, thousands used the Ouija board to contact slain loved ones. Sir Arthur Conan Doyle (author of the Sherlock Holmes mysteries) and his wife talked to their deceased son this way.

Many writers say that often their writing writes itself. The Bible, the Koran and the Bagha Vad Gita are said to be written from the "hand of God." Emerson and Beethoven both claimed that their creative essence moved through their body onto paper from an "unseen source". The Impersonal Life, written in 1916, was purported to be "channeled" on paper. In 1930, psychiatrist Virginia Moll wrote detailed reports on the power of automatic writing as a therapeutic tool. The Rhyme of the Ancient Mariner by Herman Melville was written by automatic writing as was the Urantha Book and The Course In Miracles.

Carl Jung encouraged subconscious drawing as a way to predict the future and art therapists have known for years that what we draw holds the key to inner wisdom and guidance. Many graphic artists use what they call trance art to "brainstorm" images. I may be automatic writing if something I write seems to flow outside of me, or if while doodling, my words or pictures create patterns and meanings that "tell a story".

WHAT IS AUTOMATIC WRITING AND HIERO-SCRIPTING?

"Writing is like driving at night in the fog. You can only see as far as your headlights, but you can make the whole trip that way."
– E.L. Doctorow

Automatic writing and hiero-scripting are communication forms both ancient and modern. When I learn how to do it, I easily communicate with my own subconscious mind, higher self, and profound creativity. Additionally, I can, if I choose, access deceased loved ones, past and future life images and channel guiding spirits from the "other side". It is called "automatic" because that's how it feels; as if my hand has a life of it's own.

Automatic Writing is *written* expression from a seemingly outside source. It takes various forms, from conscious journal writing at one end, to having written something and been totally unaware of that process ("trance-scripting" as if from a deep trance state) on the other. However it works for me, automatic writing is a process of self exploration. I explore the hidden terrain of my deepest self.

Hiero-Scripting, automatic painting or drawing, is the *graphic* version of automatic writing. Spontaneous images appear as simple scribbles to complex coded symbols that tell profound stories. The meaning of these mind scraps range from general to detailed and specific. The artistic or graphic expression can be as simple as one or two lines to full fledged art forms.

Much hiero-scripting can be translated into amazingly accurate answers to any of my questions. Similar to dreams, these images are lush with symbolism, humor, puns, visual slang and puzzle forms.

WHY WOULD I WANT TO DO IT?

Automatic writing and hiero-scripting are fun, enlightening and rewarding.

CAN I DO IT?

Of course I can! It's really a very simple thing to do. Anyone who can doodle, write or type can automatic write or hiero-script. I release this innate ability with little or no training and each time I do, I improve with practice. As I allow this sometimes hidden communication to flow uninhibitedly through my central nervous system onto paper or computer I explore my unlimited potentials as a human be-ing. Dreamers and dyslexics make excellent automatic writers and hiero-scripters:

Did you hear about the dyslexic atheist who didn't believe in dog? Leonardo De Vinci, Albert Einstein and Walt Disney were dyslexic. Dyslexics make terrific automatic expressionists because of their natural preference for non-linear images. This perception allows them to think more quickly and multi-dimensionally.

Intuition and automatic writing are twin sisters.
When I speak words that seem to flow on there own. Or I ask myself "Did I say that amazing thing?". When I give a massage and my hands know where to go intuitively. That's when I spontaneously experience automatic behavior. Speaking words automatically is called channeling. Moving hands automatically is called healing hands.

When I think about it, I may already be automatic writing. Was there a time that I doodled while on the phone? Wrote a letter, poetry or essay that flowed gently from me to the paper? I experience automatic writing if something I write or type seems to "write itself" or, if my words or pictures move in a pattern that tells a "story". Any time I detach or separate from my communication, and go on automatic pilot, I'm doing it!

)MATIC WRITING REAL?

I may never be 100% sure. The point of automatic writing is, for me, to explore hidden awareness and expand my consciousness in some way. If I write something that allows me to look at something in a new way, then I might use that to prove my experience is valid.

I may become emotional. For some, emotions validate their experience as real. If I feel it in my heart that may make me a believer. Or, I may get a sense that what I write is "different", then something "made up". My own unique way to verify something as real is my true test. My writing may feel "made up", or foreign and I may have a sense of detachment. This is a common experience for many. Each experience will be different, as I move in and out of various states of awareness.

It's Time To Acknowledge & De-mystify Automatic Communication.

On a recent appearances on NBC's "The Other Side" and "The Phil Donahue Show", Shelley Stockwell taught the studio and home viewer how to automatic write messages from deceased loved ones. Her simple instructions took only 3 to 4 minutes yet over 1/2 of the audience reported profound messages and listeners across the country wrote to say that they too surprised themselves with messages.

The important thing is that I allow myself to express anything, even nonsense, and not worry about sense. My right brain has an amazing way of communicating true wisdom. If I want to explore my hidden terrain through automatic writing, I just do it. I needn't worry if I "made it up". Anything I automatic write will be right!

Reality Check Exercise

It is challenging to decipher the difference between real and imagined thoughts. A way to test my perception of "reality" is by doing this simple exercise after automatically write something.

✔ I think about something that really happened and as I do, I notice what that is like for me. Where in my body do I experience this thought? How? What sensation and awareness do I associate with real? I take a deep breath and...

✔ I make up a ridiculous story about something that happened. (i.e. "At this moment I am sitting upside down, wearing a striped purple tutu and roller skates.") Again I notice what that is like for me. Where in my body do I experience this thought? How? What sensation and awareness do I associate with something that is not real.

✔ Now that I have a way to check in with my own reality, I read what I write automatically and I see how that feels to me.

A word of warning: I don't reality check something when I'm in a critical mood. My internal critic often dispels <u>all</u> information as hogwash when in control of my perception.

I BUST LIMITING ATTITUDES

Inside me live a medley of sub-personalities. Hundreds of "me's"; The angel, naughty, humorist, child, teen, mature me, old crone, seducer, prude, and the *inner critic*. The inner critic is a limiting character sometimes called Mr. or Ms. Editor.

Mr./Ms. Editor is the greatest obstacle between myself and my full creative expression. Always there to lend a hand when I need slapping down, his/her favorite phrases are things like "I can't", "You'll fail", "This is silly" and "What will people think?" It's not that Mr./Ms editor is hell bent on stomping me, It's just that he/she may have been given too much power. Mr./Ms. editor takes all the power over my thoughts and behaviors that I'm willing to give. Here's how to put them in their place:

MR./ MS. EDITOR EXERCISE

With pen or pencil in hand I write the answers to these questions with the first thing that pops into my head. Or, I answer these questions silently or out loud. I dare to give outrageously brave answers and even allow myself to verge on the ridiculous.

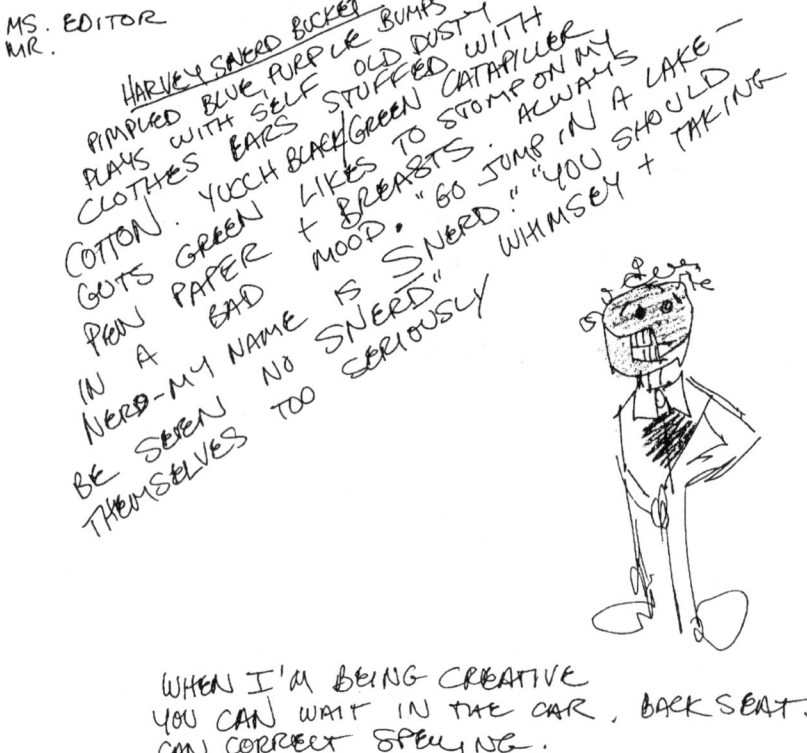

✔ I Imagine Mr./ Ms. Editor in a physical form. What is he/she like? What clothes do they wear? How do they smell. What kind of vibes do they give off? How are they built? What kind of a voice do they have? Does it sound like someone I've met before? What do they do for fun? When did Mr./Ms Editor come into my life? <u>Exactly</u> what is their job?

✔ Now that I've made mental or physical notes of this sub-personality, I thank them for doing a diligent job. I assure them that they are an important *part* of my team. But, for now, I invite them to sit in the car or wait outside the door while I let my other sub- personalities express my creativity and awareness. Perhaps they can, if they like, correct my spelling... *after* I automatic write. Maybe they'd like refine my heiro-scripting with more exacting lines..*after* I'm done. That would be fine. For now however, When I automatic write or hiero-script, they're to wait outside until I invite them in.

EXERCISE III - GUIDED IMAGERY & AUTOMATIC WRITING
(WHERE YOU WENT, WHAT KEEPS YOU FROM WRITING)

It's a big round clock. White face and bold numbers hanging on the wall of my third grade class. Mrs. Brubaker (the crusty bitch) is down the hall slamming baby's fingers into door jams. The clock ticks hours into minutes, into seconds, pushing me against the wall of home. Back to crazy mommy and the cat bashed by her broom. I am tired. I must sleep. I can visit the lands of words - my own. I can touch forever hands of love and faces too beautiful to see. Sugar rushes through my tongue. Lic-M-aids (red and green and yellow) gumming sticky upon the clock in my room. "Go to see, do ot speak" It is unspeakable her abuses. It is unthinkable. Too painful to remember.

I stick pins in my dolls stomach. Click, suck, click, suck. The rubber grabs the pin.

Abort my words.
Kill the doll.
I am too young to die.

ABRAHAM

This automatic writing message was scribed by Shelley Stockwell upon awakening in January 1995. She was to give a speech that day at a 'past life conference' below the great pyramid at Giza, Egypt. She included it in her lecture.

"I am speaking to you today because of permission given from my warden, Valerie Jacobson, of the Cairo Prison. Valerie please stand up so you may be publicly recognized. Give her a hand.

Why am I in the Cairo prison? I have committed the crime of not upholding the rule. The rule I have not upheld was that of Pharaoh. He rules and I have broken rule. My truth varied from his. My truth spoke of the pharaoh in each. He grew angry

'I am Pharaoh. How can I be in each? I talk. All listen. I have a direct line to the sun. I am the son of the sun.'

I, as scribe, said on my scrolls: 'All are pharaoh, for all can talk to the sun.'

My crime is that I have broken rule. Valerie Jacobson has a job to do; she is to punish me for my crime to not uphold the rule of her pharaoh and she does a good job. This morning she told me that I could council you today on the wisdom of Pharaoh and talk with you later, individually at the Holiday Inn (I agreed). Now she says to me and all other breakers of rule: 'No talking to the individuals; It gives too much power.'

My warden honors power. So I am here to talk to you as a group. I am here to talk about simple things like myself. I am a simple man, Abraham. I live in donkey town.

> *We eat and sleep and enjoy breath.*
> *We laugh and cry and do our best.*
> *I learned to scribe at my fathers knee*
> *Shiny eyed Joseph; man of integrity.*

To be a scribe means to place sounds upon the page, so that each, in

I AM SPEAKING TO YOU
TODAY BECAUSE OF PERMISSION ~~FOR A CERTAIN DAY~~
GIVEN BY MY WARDEN
WARDEN- VALERIE JACOBSON — FROM THE
CAIRO.
VALERIE PLEASE STAND UP S+ YOU
MAY BE PUBLICALLY RECOGNIZED
GIVE HER A HAND. WHY AM

I IN THE CAIRO PRISON
ASK? CRIME OF NOT UPHOLDING + HAVE COMMITTED ~~TAKE~~
~~LE.~~ ~~... THE PHARAOH... THE~~
~~IS~~ THE ~~I~~ HAVE NOT ~~UPHELD~~
~~IS~~ THE PHARAOH H-HEEWES ~~...~~
AND I HAVE BROKEN HIS RULE.
MY TRUTH VARIED FROM HIS.
MY TRUTH SPOKE OF THE
PHARAOH IN EACH. HE GREW
ANGRY "I AM PHAROEH. HOW
CAN I BE IN EACH?"
"I TALK ALL LISTEN, I HAVE
A DIRECT LINE TO THE SUN."
I AM THE SON OF THE SUN." ON MY
I AS SCRIBE SAID
SCROLLS "ALL ARE PHAROAH FOR
ALL CAN TALK TO THE
SUN." MY CRIME IS TO
HAVE BROKEN RULE.
VALERIE JACOBSON HAS A
JOB TO DO SHE IS TO PUNISH

Actual page from "Abraham"

turn, can lift them up and the words live again; come to life through the eyes of others. I was to place the words of my pharaoh upon the pages. You as a group, for I am told not to talk to individuals, have you a pharaoh? One who makes your rule? One who will imprison you if your rule is broken? Think now of a word of your pharaoh so you will understand this simple scribe, Abraham.

As scribe, my job is to take the words of Pharaoh and record it to the letter so no utterance shifts meaning, below my stick. Can you put down on the tablet the exact word of your Pharaoh? Pharaoh says, 'Eat happy food to break fast with sun.' And I write 'Eat Cheery Oats. I have betrayed Pharaoh.

That was my crime. I could not record the letter of the rule. I had my own ideas which interfered and I was punished for my impudence. My warden is an honorable woman. Each time she feels I trust my thoughts and words above those of Pharaoh I am punished more and more severely. Valerie Jacobson follows rules.

Each house of Pharaoh has different rules. Djoser would have asked me to speak to you today individually but my Pharaoh does not. That is all."

WHAT TO EXPECT

My writing will be more rapid, larger, and scrawlier (more cursive) than normal. Words will probably run together. Often the "i's" aren't dotted and the "t's" aren't crossed and punctuation and grammar are forgotten. Some people actually write vertically and move in patterns around the paper never having to pick up their pen while others have a staccato up and down rhythm. People often start off automatic writing illegibly, with wandering hand-writing and as they continue their hand-writing evolves and improves. I will have my own style of automatic communication and each session will take on a unique different flavor from any other time.

Pictures and words images may be clear and to the point. But most often come out as coded messages, metaphores or puzzles to be

Automatic "Backward" Writing from Jean Sheik.
To read, hold up to a mirror.

understood later; much as I might understand a dream after awakening.

My symbolic messages may be clumped together in thought patterns or interlinked as one ever flowing story. On rare occasions, I may write in a language unknown to me ("xenoescrite"- Greek "xeno" meaning foreign and french "escrite"meaning to write).

Automatic writing and Hiero- scripting are as easy as giving myself permission to let it happen, and then, letting it happen. To master automatic communication, I must give myself permission to go with the flow, let whatever happens happen; and not worry if I made it up. I will get more comfortable each time I do it.

The single most important rule for my success is to not censor, analyze, edit, or judge. I just let my "mind scraps" fall gently upon the page. Each profound and meaningful message transforms me on many levels.

RULES OF THE ROAD

If I were to enjoy a sightseeing trip in a car I would be sure that I knew how to drive that car. When I travel my precious inroads, I need to be sure that I know how to move myself through the byways.

Six basic rules keep me moving and joyous:
-     I Trust My Journey
-     Letter B
-     I Use Everything To My Best Advantage
-     I Trust My Senses
-     I Trust My Emotions
-     I Keep What I Write

✔ I Trust My Journey
Whatever information is revealed, it presents me with an opportunity to improve the condition of my life right now. God

or the higher spirit (as you envision him/her/it) at all times moves me toward joy and harmony. Each new awareness fills me with light. I become in-lightened. New awareness leaves me feeling full (full-filled), whole and satisfied. I fall in love with my life. I'm aware of your personal destiny and place in the universe. As I evolve and grow and become aware of this feeling of wholeness, I experience a profound sense of personal satisfaction.

If I experience psychic awareness during my automatic writing or hiero-scripting I enjoy it! Russell Targ and Harold Puthoff at Stanford's Research Institute proved that everyone is psychic if they simply trust the impressions they receive. Subjects told that they had "permission" to be psychic were.

✔ **Letter B**

> *Letter B*
> *Letter B*
> *Letter B*
> *Letter B*
> *There Will Be An Answer*
>
> Letter B   -Sesame Street

Everyone's technique is different. I may write with my dominant or non-dominant hand. Some people actually write with both hands "mirror style", each hand writing an entirely different message at the same time! Shelley even had a student at her Creativity Learning Institute who could automatic 'mirror' write with her feet!

There are no right or wrong ways to do automatic writing. Whatever my style, it will be perfect. I Choose the media I want to use. It may be paper and pen or typewriter. If I don't know how to type before I begin this process, I probably won't know how during the process.

✔ I Use Everything To My Best Advantage
The more I learn, the more direction and clarity I bring to living. I take advantage of knowing everything I can. I deserve it!

✔ I Trust My Senses
If I trust my senses; they respond by telling me the truth. My senses offer me health on all levels: psychic, mental, spiritual, emotional, and physical.

✔ I Trust My Emotions
Deeply emotional experiences, when expressed, relieve and relax me. Laughter and tears are powerful ways to discharge stored tension that heal. If any emotion comes up; I invite its release.

A Word Of Warning: What I Resist Persists. Holding back feelings literally dams up my nervous system, clogs my clarity and blocks my self love. Releasing trapped emotions always brings me release, relief and renewal.

✔ I Keep What I Write
"I Don't Throw These Papers Away!"

Heiro-scripting and automatic writing are sometimes expressed in cryptic messages. These symbolic communication may require a little detective work to understand. Mysterious clues give me a delightful opportunity to explore a message again and again and understand deeper meanings. I don't throw my paper away. Later I may receive a message I didn't see at first.

Each time I ponder, I gain more insight and awareness. The trick to deciphering symbolic or cryptic messages is to read it again and again. Each new look comes with fresh eyes and a new mindset. This delightful present presents itself to my present consciousness. Ah-ha, now I understand! Present means a perfect gift.

STORY OF DOLORES

"I awakened from a sound sleep when an inner voice told me the cause and the solution to all my life's struggles. Up to then I had been in emotional and physical pain and highly self destructive. "This profound massage is the key to open and heal your life. It will transform you." the voice said.

I sat up, reached for a pencil, wrote down the message and returned to sleep.

Upon reawakening, I eagerly reached for the paper:

"A band of maryaches" was scrawled across the page.

"A band of maryaches! What in the heck is that supposed to mean".

I put the paper in my purse and each day I read it. It just didn't make sense. Three weeks passed, again I read again the well worn paper.

"A band of Mary aches."

Lights flashed, I understood. My strict Catholic upbringing was underscoring the virgin Mary's pain; women's pain; my pain. Suffering succotash was her script from the scriptures! The band was, for me, marriage. Ah-ha! My painful attitudes and beliefs about life as a woman, wife and mother had influenced every problem I had. It took a while but now I make new attitudes and decisions. Enough suffering for me. It just wasn't any fun.

Thanks to this cryptic note I forgive and release those past patterns and now I re-create more positive ones.

I say these six affirmations out loud:

- ✍ **I Trust My Journey**
- ✍ **Letter B**
- ✍ **I Use Everything To My Best Advantage**
- ✍ **I Trust My Senses**
- ✍ **I Trust My Emotions**
- ✍ **I Keep What I Write**

WHAT HAPPENS IF NOTHING HAPPENS?

Practice Makes Perfect. As with anything in life, Automatic writing gets better with practice. Each time more flows forth. Sometimes, asking for a guide, loved one, or some energy from the other side to move with my pen, helps. If I do not easily do this, I don't despair. Next time will be easier. It always gets better with practice.

Hiero-scripting

As I enter, I enter into the silence. It's like being in slow motion — moving very slowly. I'm moving so slow — you can observe not only movement, but you can see the stream you... what this tells us is — wherever we go there's always an energy flow left behind us. This is what happens to all of us we're walking in each others' jet streams, & we think we're moving fast, but we're hardly moving at all. But in reality, I think we're hardly moving at all. The Great Spirit Speaks.

Automatic Writing sample signed by "The Great Spirit"

CHAPTER 2:

Automatic Writing

I'm gonna sit right down and
write myself a letter.

"If you can write a book, then you won't be able
to explain how you did it." - Joe Bob Briggs

"The whole of my published fiction should be the single-handed
product of an unseen collaborator."
- Robert Lewis Stevenson

GENERAL GUIDELINES FOR AUTOMATIC WRITING

✍ Abundance of Paper
✍ I Get Comfortable
✍ I Bless Myself
✍ I Open My Channels
✍ I Ask For Information
✍ I Write
✍ I Return To Room Awareness & Ground Myself

✔ Abundance of Paper

Abundance is the word to describe my paper. I make sure I have lots of it.

✔ I Get Comfortable

I sit comfortably in a place where I won't be disturbed.

✔ I Bless Myself

Bless me on all levels
Physically, mentall, emotionally and spiritually
So I may truly recognize and fulfill my life's purpose.
Let all teachings be for the highest good
of myself, humanity and the planet.
Help me reconnect with my special gifts
and let me lovingly shed any
negative messages given by insensitive people.
Thank you. Amen. Awomen.

✔ I Open My Channels

I Close my eyes and imagine going to a beautiful place. Somewhere that brings me a feeling of peace and serenity. I enjoy this place from my sense of smell, taste, touch, sound and sight. I imagine entering a special room that I design; just the way I like it. Waiting there is my own personal guide. My guide is any I choose to imagine. I relax in this special place with this special friend.

My guide hands me a sacred computer disk. "This disk comes from the automatic writing archives of the Akashic Records Library" they say. "Upon it are all the secrets of automatic communication, all the wisdom of those who have gone before and all those to come receive it and place it into your deepest mind with your next breathe." I take a deep breath and place these sacred messages into my deepest mind.

✔ I Ask For Information

Exploration I may choose to write with no structure or I ask for specific information like: What is my life's purpose? How can I create more abundance? How can I improve the quality of my life? Automatic writing too is a great way to "brainstorm" for personal goal setting. And to tap my unlimited creativity.

Guidance I may ask for guidance from God or Spirit. I can request a message from the living or the deceased (loved one, a friend, a famous person, a past life). I may "regress" back into my childhood in this lifetime to clarify something I've blocked or forgotten. Information from the past helps me understand, heal and fulfill my life's purpose.

Regression/Progression I can "progress" into the future in this lifetime or another; pinpoint a specific space in time or randomly explore. I can automatic write poetry, short stories or books. Many scriptwriters use this technique to create and enhance their work.

Whatever I choose, I allow information to emerge from my deepest wisdom without censor. I can decipher and make sense of it later.

Destinations For Automatic Writing:
✐ I explore my deepest mind
✐ I answer my questions
✐ I tap my unlimited creativity

✍ I time travel

✍ I contact the deceased

✍ I channel my guides

✔ **I Write**

I take a deep, full breath, all that my lungs can comfortably hold, and I gently let it out. I do not judge, analyze or think. I'm not concerned if it makes sense because it might not. I decide to write whatever comes. As I begin, I let all impulses move through my nervous system to the pen and onto the page. I Let my pen move as if it had a life of it's own and let whatever comes come. At first, I might write my question or the name of any energy or person I wish to contact. Then I scribble, doodle, draw lines, shapes or random words. I let them flow. No matter what, I don't stop. I continue to move words or record my random thoughts. Eventually, I will find messages - lots of them.

✔ **I Return To Room Awareness and Ground Myself**

I say 'thank you' and I return to a fully alert state of mind by taking a cleansing breath, shaking out my hands and imagining energy draining through my palms and through the bottom of my feet into the earth. Or I can wash my hands, eat something or drink a glass of water.

AUTO SUGGESTIONS FOR AUTOMATIC WRITING

Another way to automatic write is to listen to Shelley Stockwell's Automatic Writing Journey cassette or to record and play back my voice speaking the following set of instructions. I can play soft music in the background if I like.

"I bless myself on all levels making sure that all of these teachings are for my highest good. I put my feet on the floor. Take a deep breath through my body (pause) and let it out. (pause) One more breath to the brain. Let it go. I Close my eyes.

I imagine myself programmed with an automatic communications disk that allows me to flow words on paper. I let the words move through my right or left hand. I flow words on paper. I don't think, analyze, editor judge: just simply let the words put themselves across the page. I'm not concerned if they make sense. They may not at first. I don't have to cross my t's or dot my i's if I don't want to. I may write any way that happens; up or down, top or bottom. It doesn't matter. I just write.

I take another deep breath. (pause) Let it out. (pause) Put my pen upon the paper as I let the words out. Mind scraps, I write mind scraps helter skelter, naturally falling as they will. And I continue to relax, breath and write. Good."

SPECIAL DESTINATIONS FOR AUTOMATIC WRITING

- ✍ I explore my deepest mind
- ✍ I answer my questions
- ✍ I tap my unlimited creativity
- ✍ I travel time
- ✍ I contact the deceased
- ✍ I channel my guides

I EXPLORE MY DEEPEST MIND

I hold within my being a profound inner wisdom. This part of myself knows all I need to do to make my life perfect on all levels: physically, mentally, emotionally and spiritually. It hold in it's memory-banks every thing that has ever happened to me and everything that is to happen to me! It know exactly what that each moment is like for me from the point of view of each of my senses. At any given moment, this marvelous part of me knows the truth of everything and everyone around me. The trick is to tap it. And automatic writing is beautiful door into this deepest knowing.

Free For All Exercise

✍ Abundance of Paper

✍ I Get Comfortable

✍ I Bless Myself

✍ I Write For 10 Minutes Without Stopping

✍ I Return To Room Awareness & Ground Myself

✔ Abundance of Paper

Abundance is the word to describe my paper. I make sure I have lots of it.

✔ I Get Comfortable

I sit comfortably in a place where I won't be disturbed.

✔ I Bless Myself

Bless me on all levels
Physically, mentally
Emotionally and spiritually
So I may truly
recognize and fulfill my life's purpose.
Let all teachings be for the highest good
of myself, humanity and the planet.
Help me reconnect
with my special gifts
and let me lovingly shed any
negative messages given by insensitive people.
Thank you.
Amen. Awomen

✔ I Write For 10 Minutes Without Stopping

I commit to write for 10 minutes no matter what! I

write from my stream of consciousness random words upon my page..I let my pencil or fingers go. Some folks like to run around the room first or sing or tone to get in a loose mood. The important thing is that I don't stop writing words once I begin.

✔ I Return To Room Awareness And Read

I read what I wrote. I may have to look past the deadwood or ramblings to return to the essence of my message but it's all there if I focus in. I save these gems. They often take on new meanings each time I read them. What are the messages I see? If I want, I repeat the last two assignments.

I ANSWER MY QUESTIONS

I let it flow
I let it go
I answer questions
I want to know.

Automatic communication opens the energy of my mental transmissions to the page. Any questions I have are easily answered since my deepest wisdom can tap my very genetic coding which holds all the information about every part of my being. My answers may be cryptic or complicated.

Muster a Cluster Exercise

Muster a cluster lets me brainstorn to clarify my dreams and goals and the steps I can take to real-eyes them.

- ✍ Abundance of Paper
- ✍ I Get Comfortable
- ✍ I Bless Myself
- ✍ I Write My Question
- ✍ I Circle a Key Word in the middle of my page
- ✍ I Cluster Words Around It
- ✍ I Write a Statement of my Original Question
- ✍ I Return To Room Awareness & Ground Myself

✔ Abundance of Paper

Abundance is the word to describe my paper. I make sure I have lots of it.

✔ I Get Comfortable

I sit comfortably in a place where I won't be disturbed.

✔ I Bless Myself

Bless me on all levels
Physically, mentally, emotionally and spiritually
So I may truly recognize and fulfill my life's purpose.
Let all teachings be for the highest good of myself, humanity and the planet.
Help me reconnect with my special gifts as I write words upon my page.
And let me lovingly shed any negative messages given by insensitive people.
Thank you. Amen. Awomen

✔ I Write My Question

At the top of blank piece of paper I
write the question that I want answered.ie:

> What is Zen?
> What is an angel

What are the Pliadies
What is the meaning of my life?
How do I make $300,000 this year?

✔ I Circle a Key Word In The Middle Of My Page

In big letters I write or print the key word from my question.ie:

Zen
angel
pliadies
my life
$300,000

✔ I Cluster Words Around It

I take a deep breath and write random words around my central word. Anything that pops into my mind. I circle these thoughts and connect any words to them that come tome or go back to my central circle and add more words.

✔ I Write a Statement of My Original Question

On a new piece of paper and write a statement using the key words from my original question.I write anything that pops into my mind without editing.ie:

Zen is:
an angel is:
Pliedies are:
meaning of my life is
I make $300,00 next year by.....

✔ I Return To Room Awareness And Ground Myself

I TAP MY UNLIMITED CREATIVITY

A fun way to tap my creative genius is to imagine that I am a famous creative genius that I admire. I imagine that I am E.E. Cummings, Plato, Picasso, Michaelangelo and I write from their vibration.

I TRAVEL TIME

"The collective unconscious contains the whole spiritual heritage of mankind's evolution, born anew in the brain structure of every individual."
-Carl Jung

Where Will I Travel?

I decide what I'd like to know, explore, or clarify. Will I go back in time (regression)? Will I explore my birth, past lives, or the source of an issue or pain? Am I tracking another to see what our relationship was in another place in time? Am I choosing to go into the future (progression)? How far into the future? Next week? Next month? Five years from now? 100 years? Am I looking to meet an inner guide? Choosing to heal an illness? Alter a pattern of behavior that does not serve me well? Or, do I decide not to decide and go anywhere the journey takes me? Whatever I choose, it will be perfect. Once I plan my course, I begin.

I can easily access:

✍ Past Lives (regression)

✍ Future Lives (progression)

✍ Between lives (ascension)

Where do Past and Future Life Images Come From?

How little is known of my mind. My mind understanding itself is sometimes a heartbeat away from my grasp. That's why learning to time travel is so fascinating. Past life theorists say that other life time and between life images come from keen imagination, reincarnation or the collective unconscious. When I explore powerful scenarios of other people, places and times; I judge for myself.

Are Past Lives A Product Of Genetics?

Shelley's friend, Roxanne was born with a white streak in the front of her black hair, a striking characteristic that her mother had as well. When her child was born, she too sported that same white lock of hair. What physical characteristics do I reflect from my Ancestors?

Every cell in my body is an identical genetically coded replica of every other cell complete with my family records of eye color, strengths and weaknesses. Does each cell also carry detailed information about the lives of my ancestors?

What Do These Images Do For Me?

Time travel bring me into a more intimate harmony with myself, my life's purpose and all humankind. I can use it to heal physical and emotional blocks or pain, explore my relationships with others, and to learn more about what makes me tick. Images of remembered lives are like holograms. I may look at them from various angles and perspectives and they'll change in impact, hue, and intensity.

Each image overlays my life in the present. Each helps me take control of my actions in the "now". When I'm unconsciously influenced by an event, I act to recreate it or avoid it. Both of these re-actions determine my action. When I remember the source of my re-action, I empower myself I no longer need to behave "because of" or "in spite of". My action is a decision based on my clarity and free will.

HOW TO AUTOMATIC WRITE OTHER PLACES IN TIME

- ✍ Abundance of Paper
- ✍ I Get Comfortable
- ✍ I Bless Myself
- ✍ I Open My Channels
- ✍ I Ask For Information
- ✍ I Write

✔ **Abundance of Paper**
Abundance is the word to describe my paper. I make sure I have lots of it.

✔ **I Get Comfortable**
I sit comfortably in a place where I won't be disturbed.

✔ I Bless Myself

Bless me on all levels; physically, mentally, emotionally and spiritually
So I may truly recognize and fulfill my life's purpose
Let all teachings be for the highest good of myself, humanity and the planet.
Help me reconnect with my special gifts as I automatically write words upon my page.
And let me lovingly shed any negative messages given by insensitive people.
Thank you. Amen. Awomen

✔ I Focus my Attention On My Breath

I become aware of my breathing and notice that I have my own distinct rhythm, energy and vibration. My vibration is unique. In all the history of all the world there is not another who holds this identical vibration. I might notice any sights, sounds, rhythms, tastes, smells and sensations that come to me now.

✔ I Focus my Attention On My Destination

I turn my attention now to my past. Do I want to go to another lifetime? Do I want to go back in time to another place in this current lifetime to explore it more fully and remember? Do I want to go into the future? Or discover where I was between lifetimes? Do I want to track a relationship or a physical pain? I decide. Then I take a deep breath and relax.

✔ I Write

Relaxing my hands, I simply write without censoring or editing. Whatever I write or draw will be perfect. If I like I can say the following words as spring boards:

> Feet?
> Clothes?
> Senses?
> Others?
> Location?

Time?
Experience?
Death?
White Light
Learned then?
Learned now?

AUTO SUGGESTIONS FOR AUTOMATIC WRITING

Another way to travel time is to record and play back the following set of instructions accompanied by soft recorded music.

"I sit comfortably and bless myself on all levels; physically, mentally, spiritually and emotionally; making sure that all of these teachings are for my highest good. I take a deep cleansing breath to my body my body. (pause). Let it out. (pause) One more breath to the mind. (pause) Let it go. I Close my eyes and relax my eyelids so much that they just don't feel like opening. I imagine myself programmed with a solar disc that allows me to flow words upon paper. I know that I can easily let the words move through my right or left hand. I don't think, analyze, editor judge: just simply let the words put themselves across the page. I'm not concerned if it makes sense, it may, it may not, all is well.

I now imagine myself moving down a corridor of time to the past, or future or any specific place in time that I would like to explore. Along the corridor are many doorways; each to another life time where I learned valuable lessons that affect my life now. I find the door that draws me and I enter.

I remember to keep breathing. I put my pen upon the paper as I let the words out. This is called mind scraps. While I write mind scraps, I take deep, full breaths."

3 PAST LIFE REGRESSIONS FROM SHELLEY STOCKWELL

(From her book
Time Travel: The Do-It-Yourself Past Life Journey Handbook
Creativity Unlimited Press, Rancho Palos Verdes CA., 90275)

GARY OLDSTEN

Gary Oldsten of the great greenest of Greenland. Open to sea, sand, standing alone by the sea, my sea made for me. Seaweed, shells, I like to walk upon the sand. Cold grains in my toes, I will die barefoot of cold before I am old. I am always slightly alone. My right foot gimp, drags sand trails to the sea. Pop the seaweed poppers, that's my music calamity.

My mothers, has yellow hair like pale lemons in the sun, long days in the sun. White walls n my island in Greek lands. Small and tidy, my island. Abraxus is it's name. I eat pomegranates and paint my gimp foot red. Octopus and squid are rare delights. My mouth drips with oozo and squid. My father likes to dance in the hall with red-lipped lady of the night. His hair is white & smells of pipe. My dog is gray and stupid and fine. I have a lip tucked tight above and speak tight and my teeth hurt, lowers crushed upon uppers to my nose. I am alone on my sandy beach looking at a million stars. I die on this beach from drinking salt and learn that I have melted sand. I reach a silent beach.

BISON

How do you do this and that. How do you go into and out of awareness and don't care. I am holy holy holy. Jaw tight, throat tight, going in and out of buffalo. Buffalo horns upon my head, my crown for (king to some) buffalo prince in our land of smoke mountains and sage caves. My head hurts. Like the bison I wear I have to suffer for my food. The bison gave his life. I wear his horns and head upon my own. His life is within me. Food from the great white clouds, food of life runs through the river, the sun. The bison up from now to forever. The bison and man locked like interlaced branches of trees. Like finger on hands. Bison God. Bison Food. Bison Life.

THE GIRL IN THE MIDDLE

I am going to die. Oh, why must I die?
I love living clinging upon me
like spider webs tickling my nose
I want to feel the grass in my toes.

The pollen is strong;
(yellow crumbs of life sprinkled on little bee legs)
I want to be.
I want to stay sprinkled on earth.
I don't want to go or leave you; (you of my heart)
You are my heart.
I have struggled to love this body (where I dwell)
This body which transports my heart and soul and thoughts.
I don't want you to leave me, body,
after we finally got to love again.

If I go (torn from you)
what will become of our dreams?
Our visions of tomorrows?
Our time to laugh
and our deep sorrows?

I have no control and I want to control.
I want to choose that I have no choice.
I have no choice.

I want to go back
back to the years of tender corn
(waving in fields, steamy and warm)
back to the earth
(hot, mud parched, dry)
back to mama and apple pie.

Back to the checkered table cloth
and coffee (black as sin)
back to the swing (the big white swing)
creaky in the hot summer night.
Sweat smells sweet like tea.

And the children in white frocks
skip-the-loop upon the brown grass.

Jonas, Becky come to the fair.
The barker came. The clown is there.
Joelly and Barbara and Cary Ann,
will take you back where everyone can
dance and swing and play the fiddle
and I can love the girl in the middle.

Why do I write this gibber posh pie?
Why am I in this stew?
Tell me what is wrong with me.
What am I to do?
So give me a plum cake and apple flap
and I will give you my love back.

I CONTACT THE DECEASED

A molecule moving in the dark of night
Silently entering beyond my sight
Surging in rhythm with my heart
I am the whole
I am a part.

Departed loved ones from the other side are easy to contact and their messages can often be profoundly moving. I decide who I'd like to contact and what, if anything specific, I'd like to explore. Or, do I decide not to decide and contact one who is willing to communicate? Whatever I choose, it will be perfect. Once I plan my course, I begin.

I can easily contact:
- Departed loved ones
- Departed with unfinished business
- Historical figures
- Friendly ghosts

How to Automatic Write Deceased Loved Ones

- ✍ Abundance of Paper
- ✍ I Get Comfortable
- ✍ I Bless Myself
- ✍ I Focus Upon My Breath
- ✍ I Focus Upon My Loved One
- ✍ I Ask Them To Communicate
- ✍ I Write
- ✍ I Return To Room Awareness And Ground Myself

✔ Abundance of Paper
Abundance is the word to describe my paper. I make sure I have lots of it.

✔ I Get Comfortable
I sit comfortably in a place where I won't be disturbed.

✔ I Bless Myself
Bless me on all levels
Physically, mentally, emotionally and spiritually
So I may truly recognize and fulfill my life's purpose
Let all teachings be for the highest good of myself, humanity and the planet.
Help me reconnect with my special gifts and let me lovingly shed any negative messages given by insensitive people.
Thank you. Amen. Awomen

✔ I Focus My Attention On My Breath
I become aware of my breathing and notice that I have my own distinct rhythm, energy and vibration. My vibration is unique. In all the history of all the world I am the only one who holds this identical vibration. I notice any sights, sounds, rhythms, tastes, smells and sensations that come to me now.

✔ I Turn My Attention To A Deceased Loved One
I turn my attention now to the person I want to contact. I

notice their energy, vibration, rhythm, colors, textures, sounds tastes and smells. I let my mind and awareness wrap themselves about this departed one. I can imagine them in physical body or as a spirit, either is fine.

✔ I Ask Them To Communicate

Relaxing my hands, I invite them to give me a message or answer a specific question. Sometimes, writing their name over and over again works well

✔ I Write

✔ I Return To Room Awareness And Ground Myself

SISTERS AUTOMATIC WRITE THEIR DECEASED MOTHER

Lisa Marie: "When I automatic write, I receive messages from my deceased mother. The first time I felt her presence I said to myself. "Mom if you have something to say, why don't you say it now as I write."

I receive her messages in my hand and then my hand is kind of guided along as I write. Now, when I feel her around me, I definitely feel her hand when she's ready to write. I can be thinking about something else and my hand plops down on the page and that's it."

Susan: "When Lisa Marie showed me her writing, just from the look of it and the way it felt I knew it was my Mom. I immediately started crying just from the look of it. I knew it was no way possible it was anyone else. I knew it was my Mom. A few weeks later I tried and I started to do it too."

I CHANNEL MY GUIDES

Channeling is the way I express my higher, source self or guides. Healing, intuition, inspiration, creativity, and psychic awareness are all forms of channeling. When I know that something is going to happen before it does or see a bigger picture I am generally channeling. Channeling opens me to information that, may not be consciously known to me.

Channeling my guides will positively change my energy and I will feel more complete. It is very rewarding. I feel great when I channel my guides.

There are no taboo questions. As a matter of fact, energies that come through me love all questions. Each unique personality enthusiastically answers questions about the past, present and future and teaches me the lessons of unconditional love and overcoming fear. The information that comes from spirit guidance is generally very accurate and psychic. It could however, be inaccurate. Any information that I receive is just more information that I can use for my entertainment, growth and awareness. If it doesn't resonate or vibrate as correct, I simply let it go.

I can easily access:
 ✍ Guardian Angels
 ✍ Guiding Spirits
 ✍ Ascended Masters

<u>**AUTOMATIC WRITING BY KENDRA**</u>
as channeled by Shelley Lessin Stockwell

What is a channeling?
Channeling is an energy exchange between a human (or animal) and spirit. The channel is a portal, a doorway, between dimensions of consciousness. This doorway swings in both directions. For humans, channeling allows them to remember their essence and ancestry. For spirits, channeling allows other dimensions or realms of consciousness (spirit) an opportunity to

resonate in a physical body. This for us is an all-together enjoyable vibration or interchange.

Why would spirit choose to lower vibration and visit an earthling?

<u>SPIRITUAL INTERCOURSE</u>

You've got the body
We add the spirit
You experience spirit
We experience body

For us, we reflect ourselves and our own history through your physicality. We, of altered dimension (or as we call ourselves, "earth connected spirits"), are teachers. We believe that for you to know about your essence, origins and structure you must also know your future. We come to you as a fragment of your future, so you may know your essence in the marrow. We think that then, the you of the future and we of spirit, will enjoin in an harmonic exchange. We find our encounters with you joyous, instructive and beautiful. And so do you.

Who are you?
You might think of us as energy freaks. Our bumper sticker would read "Spirit does it with frequency."- just kidding.

Talk to me about aging
To age is to return to full vibration (full spectrum) and recall ones origins and future. From our point of view, one never ages or loses vibration. Even in your physical plane, even in illness or what you call death, humans are an eternal vibration. Aging may refine your vibration causing a more tightly calibrated energy tonality or it may return you anew to full vibration. Think of your life as tones of a scale, or colors of a spectrum. Your job is to sound each note of natural vibration. or shine each color.

The baby is born in full spectrum or tonality and he resonates full on his own accord because she is newly returned from our dimension. The training and rituals of others often put this fullness of energy and color below raps or stifling units and the child grows to specialize only in certain tones.

As one ripens by age, permission, spirit or guidance, a person often returns to full spectrum or tonality. Artists of life, younger ones and those who have, what you call "near death experiences", those who are restricted in movement, and the aged, often resonate fully.

Is channeling real? or does the channel make it up?

Are thoughts real? Do you make up the colors you see, the sounds you hear, the tastes you taste, the stirring in your heart or the laughter? Of course not. Each is as natural as breathing. To live is to allow the energy of life's expression to flow through you. Life flowing through you is spirit or channeling.

Focus your attention or perception upon your body and notice how you feel at this moment. Focus upon your mind and notice that you are thinking. This is challenging for you to think about thinking. It is like wrapping a mist about a mist. Now focus your attention upon spirit energy and you will notice its presence (presents) also.

To resonate or dwell simultaneously in the 3 stratas; body, mind and spirit, is to sing your song in full spectrum. Together you that you are whole-holy.

"Drawing was a life-long dream. Then in Nov. '95, I felt compelled to get pencil and paper. To my amazement, I found the lines already on the paper. I could see the picture so I just drew in the shadows as they appeared to me."

– Persis Newland

How to Automatic Write My Guides: Happy Mediums

- ✍ Abundance of Paper
- ✍ I Get Comfortable
- ✍ I Bless Myself
- ✍ I Focus my Attention On My Breath
- ✍ I Vibrate My Chakras
- ✍ I Ask for my Guidance
- ✍ I Write

✔ **Abundance of Paper**
Abundance is the word to describe my paper. I make sure I have lots of it.

✔ **I Get Comfortable**
I sit comfortably in a place where I won't be disturbed.

✔ **I Bless Myself**
Bless me on all levels
Physically, mentally, emotionally and spiritually
So I may truly recognize and fulfill my life's purpose
and let all teachings be for the highest good of myself and humanity.
Help me reconnect with my special gifts and let me lovingly shed any negative messages given by insensitive people.
Thank you. Amen. Awomen

✔ **I Focus my Attention On My Breath**
I become aware of my breathing and notice that I have my own distinct rhythm, energy and vibration. My vibration is unique. In all the history of all the world there is not another who holds this identical vibration. I might notice any colors, sounds, rhythms, tastes and smells that come to me with this awareness.

✔ I Vibrate My Chakras

I close my eyes and I become aware of my breathing and breath to the base of my spine and hold it in for a moment. Then, with the out breath I "Ohm" vibrating myself from bottom to top. Any vibration that flows easily is perfect. Or I breath in with the word "hun" and out with "sah". Whichever I choose, I imagine that light enters my crown chakra and fills me with bright whiteness. Some folks see flashing lights behind their closed eyes. I may have a feel a rush, as if I leave my body or I may feel quite normal and think that I make it all up. Each perception is fine.

✔ I Ask for my Guidance

I summon my guide by a specific name if I know it. Writing the name again and again works well for some. Or I simply invite spirit for a message.

✔ I Write

Relaxing my hands, I simply write without censoring or editing. Whatever I write or draw will be perfect.

SANDI AUTOMATIC WRITES HER SPIRIT GUIDE

I type the name of my spirit guide repeatedly "Aswana, Aswana, Aswana" or I type a phrase "Breath in love. Breath in love." that she gave me. This gives my rational mind a focus and it turns off. The next thing I know, my hands are typing.

HOW TO USE PSYCHOMETRY

Psychometry is the art of holding or touching a physical object and picking up information about others who have touched or worn it.

- ✍ Abundance of Paper
- ✍ I Get Comfortable
- ✍ I Bless Myself
- ✍ I Hold or Touch The Object I Am "Reading"
- ✍ I Ask My Guides For Information
- ✍ I Write

✔ **Abundance of Paper**

Abundance is the word to describe my paper. I make sure I have lots of it.

✔ **I Get Comfortable**

I sit comfortably in a place where I won't be disturbed.

✔ **I Bless Myself**

Bless me on all levels
Physically, mentally, emotionally and spiritually
So I may truly recognize and fulfill my life's purpose
and let all teachings be for the highest good of myself and humanity.
Help me reconnect with my special gifts and let me lovingly shed any negative messages given by insensitive people.
Thank you. Amen. Awomen

✔ **I Hold or Touch The Object I Am "Reading"**

✔ **I Ask My Guides For Information**

✔ **I Write**

AUTO SUGGESTIONS FOR GUIDED MESSAGES

Another way to channel write is to record in my own voice the following set of instructions accompanied by soft recorded music.

"I sit comfortably. as I bless myself on all levels physically, mentally, spiritually and emotionally, making sure that all of these teachings are for my highest good. I Take a deep breath and cleanse my body my body.(pause). Let it out. One more breath to the brain. Let it go. I Close my eyes and relax my eyelid so much that they just don't feel like opening.

I imagine myself programmed with a solar disc that allows me to flow words from spirit upon paper. I know that I can easily let the words move through my right or left hand. I don't think, analyze, editor judge: just simply let the words put themselves across the page. I'm not concerned if it makes sense, it may not that's fine.

I now imagine myself being lifted in wings that guide me to write. I take another deep breath. Let it out. Put my pen upon the paper as I let the words out. This is called mind scraps. While I write mind scraps, I take another full breath."

A Message from Archangel Michael

"Let us not mince the words, it is the seven survival essences you request. All is a process of life and death but it is the survival essences you request. For a human to survive they must:

1. **Fuel** *with sun (warmth) water, air and rest. They must:*

2. **Perpetuate Their Species** *with sex and teaching their young*

3. **Release Energy** *with movement, laughter tears and elimination*

4. **Have Purpose** *need to be needed (succor), be part of, recognized, to be productive*

5. **Re•Member** *(all genetic memory) Their origin (spirit), their structure (body) and earth memory (mind)*

6. **Contact Others** *Love, touch and companionship*

7. **Evolve** *Die, grow and expand, rip and kill, love and nurture, live and die (all cells, ideas and body package)*

HOW TO AUTOMATIC WRITE MY DEEPEST MIND

✎ Abundance of Paper
✎ I Get Comfortable
✎ I Bless Myself
✎ I Focus my Attention On My Breath
✎ I Vibrate My Chakras
✎ I Call Upon My Inner Wisdom and Higher Self
✎ I Write

✔ Abundance of Paper
Abundance is the word to describe my paper. I make sure I have lots of it.

✔ I Get Comfortable
I sit comfortably in a place where I won't be disturbed.

✔ I Bless Myself
Bless me on all levels
Physically, mentally, emotionally and spiritually
So I may truly recognize and fulfill my life's purpose
Let all teachings be for the highest good of myself, humanity and the planet.
Help me reconnect with my special gifts and let me lovingly shed any negative messages given by insensitive people.
Thank you. Amen. Awomen

✔ I Focus my Attention On My Breath

I become aware of my breathing and notice that I have my own distinct rhythm, energy and vibration. My vibration is unique. In all the history of all the world there is not another who holds this identical vibration. I might notice any colors, sounds, rhythms, tastes and smells that come to me with this awareness.

✔ I Vibrate My Chakras

I close my eyes and I become aware of my breathing and breath to the base of my spine and hold it in for a moment. Then, with the out breath I "Ohm" vibrating myself from bottom to top. Any vibration that flows easily is perfect. Or I breath in with the word "hun" and out with "sah". Whichever I choose, I imagine that light enters my crown chakra and fills me with bright whiteness.

I think and imagine myself in a spotlight of light . Within this light is my auric field, my past, my present, my future, all my experience and guidance. This is my energy. It belongs uniquely to me. And I relax

✔ I Call Upon My Inner Wisdom and Higher Self

I ask for a message from the part of myself that knows all of my answers: knows exactly what I need to do to make my life work perfectly physically, mentally, emotionally and spiritually.

✔ I Write

Relaxing my hands, I simply write without censoring or editing. Whatever I write or draw will be perfect.

"Relationships" by Stephanie (age 12)

Heiroscripted Dream Chart

CHAPTER 3:

Hiero-
Scripting

A picture is worth a thousand words.

GENERAL GUIDELINES FOR HIERO-SCRIPTING

Teacher: "What are you drawing?"
Child: "I'm drawing a picture of God."
Teacher: "But no one knows what God looks like."
Child: "They will when I'm done"

A picture's worth a thousand words.
Pictures go to the heart of my inner self communication. Sketchy and wise; hiero-scripting, or automatic drawing, capture my thoughts as images. When I interpret the pictures I create, I need to be patient since mind images are symbolic and often archtypal.

A good way to interpret their meaning is to view each part of my drawing as it relates to the whole. What colors did I choose? What parts are bold or timid? Where did I place them on the page?..How detailed or significant are the elements of my drawing? How does my drawing relate to my life?

Doing the same assignment more than once and comparing their sameness and differences also give me profound insight. Re-creating negative images into positive ones affirms positive change in my life.

Repaint and thin no more.
If I find my symbols weak or too negative I move myself to a happier ending by re-painting a new image. When I re-create a scene with a new picture of health and happiness my subconscious assists me to make it so.

When I analyze my images it's important that I don't refer to dream analysis books or take anyone else's word for it. After all, I know best. Important things to observe while interpreting my images is any angry, frightened, joyous, peaceful; any depictions that have impact on me emotionally. If I repeat an exercise any symbols that repeat or change in the tone, size, shape, or color should be noted.

A word of warning I don't over interpret these gems: I look, linger, analyze, release and live.

I TAP MY DEEPEST MIND

My mind thinks in images; a collage of colors, shapes, tones and patterns. I can easily place these upon my page as symbolic representations of who I really am. These inner symbols of myself are the basis of all written and spoken language. For language is simply an agreement that certain lines or sounds represent a certain symbolic meaning. As I scribe these picture symbols in a natural, random way; each individual symbol, and the order in which they form, tell true stories from my inner wisdom. Consciously interpreting their meanings is fun and fascinating.

What Do These Images Do For Me?

Art Therapists use many of these simple techniques as a therapeutic tool to help their clients better connect with their true feelings. With hiero-scripting I become my own art therapist and this inner communication brings to light inner my conflicts and strengths and lets me hear the voice of my inner self. It's generally easier for me to interpret my inner consciousness than anyone else.

In recent years Dr. Bernie Siegel and O. Carl Simonton popularized drawing and color techniques to assist critically ill patients to identify, heal and integrate the mind-body connection. Hiero-scripting taps my dream place as a visual representation.. From these subconscious images I identify anger, conflict, joy and love.

Case Study

Wall paintings found in the Ardéche region of France have been traced back some 20,000 years. The animals depicted tell vivid stories about life.

RULES OF THE ROAD

Comfort and Good Posture.

The better my posture the more blood goes to the septum Pellucidum (or Lucidum) and the more creative I become. No need to crane my neck over my playsheets. A flat, sturdy surface to draw upon is important too. I make sure That I am physically comfortable and I begin.

Just Do It!

It's important that I don't analyze my creations *while* I do them. This is not an exercise in art. It is an exercise in self expression. I leave Mr./Ms Critic in the car. Later, I return with fresh eyes and see what I see, I can ask Mr./Ms Critic or a friend to put in their two bits. I don't analyze my drawing to death. It may not even make sense or appear "normal". Oh well.

I Go With The Flow.

Hiero-scripting is a journey not a destination. I have available what ever medium I enjoy; crayons, pen, charcoal, paint. When I begin I let my hand (some prefer their feet and Jai Kwong of Korea uses his privates) relax and draw in slow motion. I allow any pictures, even vague and random ones, to gently glide upon my page. If I want to write words or labels on my drawing that's fine. Mainly, I detach from my hand and what it is drawing. When you get good at this it becomes a sublime out of body experience!

WHAT DO MY MESSAGES MEAN?

To interpret my hiero-scripts I need to observe four things about their composition and the elements: the size, the spatial relationships, the colors and the images. I can explore the meaning alone, with a friend or with a helping professional.

Space Cadet.

My placement of images and color on the page and their inter-relationship, one to the other, enhances my conscious understanding. How does each part relate to the whole? How much of the paper or canvas did I use? If I'm hiero-scripting a person, myself for example, what size did I make me? How large the image generally indicates how good I felt about my subject at that moment. Usually, the larger the better. So I notice how large one part of my drawing is compared to another part.

Are the images on the right or left of the page? Images on the left sometimes mean the past, the subconscious, the right or female side of the brain, and, occasionally, means that I don't like what's going on. If a head or eyes faces right may indicate a bright future and that everything is going well by my standards. Images that move from right to left mean that things are progressing in a positive way. If I am left handed or hiero-scripted with my left hand this left to right analysis would be reversed.

A fun way to analyze my drawing is to assign each quadrant a meaning ie:

Top Left FUTURE	Top Right PRESENT
Bottom Left PAST	Bottom Right VERY NEAR FUTURE

Spectrum Speculation.

The colors I choose often indicate where I stand. Is my graphic dark or light? Heavy or airy? Bold or timid? The following color keys to my kingdom is a broad guideline only. I know better than any one else what my colors represent for me.

Color Keys to My Kingdom

Black: Grief, sadness, depression, assertion, definition. If black is on the bottom of my hiero-script or on the feet of myself or another it may mean that I don't like what's going on at the moment.

White: enlightenment, the unknown, hidden information. If I drew with a white crayon on a white paper I may be hiding something from myself that needs to be uncovered

Pink and Pastel Tones: Softness, timidity, babies

Silver: Intuitive, cycles, often relates to the moon and planets

Red: Strong feelings, passion, power, pain, danger, action or simply colors of real life like an apple, a heart or blood.

Purple: Spirituality, power, peace

Orange: Change, renewal, communication, focus

Yellow and Gold: Enlightenment, energy, life giving, support, intellect. A sunrise often means renewal, a sunset; change or ending

Green,and Brown: Earth, life, renewal , new growth, potential, healing money (in the USA)

Blue: Peace, tranquility, spirituality, everything's gonna be O.K.

How do friends analyze the meaning of hieroglyphs?

If I explain to my friend the meaning of my hiero-script I clarify what I see. To make this easy, I imagine that I am the greatest art therapist or art historian in the world. I point out the elements and the bigger pictures of my work. I tell my friend how these images relate to my life.

Next, I let my friend share what they see. A loving friend always sees with fresh eyes what I may miss. If what they say fits I take it in. If not I let it go.

If my friend asks me to interperet their piece of expression, I get centered and report what I see. I trust my awareness. Asking questions is good, too. i.e. "What were you thinking or feeling when you drew this?" It's a good idea to avoid dream or symbolic analysis books.

Hieroscripting by Shelley

HOW TO HEIRO-SCRIPT

- ✏ Paper, Pens, Crayons, Paints
- ✏ Style and Destination
- ✏ I Get Comfortable
- ✏ I Bless Me
- ✏ I Open My Channels
- ✏ I Ask For Information
- ✏ I Create

✔ Paper, Pens, Crayons, Paints

I choose my medium. Will I use pen on paper, paints, or crayons? Abundance is the word here. I make sure I have lots of paper and colors if I want to use them. A box of crayons with 24 colors is great.

✔ Style and Destination

Will I use the format of a mandala or other geometric design? Or will I allow my journey to unfold with no structure?

✔ I Get Comfortable

I sit comfortably, with good posture, where I won't be disturbed.

✔ I Bless Me

Bless me on all levels
Physically, mentally, emotionally and spiritually
So I may truly recognize and fulfill my life's purpose
and let all teachings be for the highest good of myself and humanity.
Help me reconnect with my special gifts and let me lovingly shed any negative messages given by insensitive people.
I choose to have my answers during this session come in the form of pictures.
Thank you. Amen. Awomen.

✔ **I Open My Channels**

I Close my eyes and imagine going to a beautiful place in nature. Somewhere that brings me a feeling of peace and serenity. Experience this place from any one or all of my senses. Enjoy the smells, colors, tastes, breezes, and sights. Now I imagine going into a special room (I am the designer). Waiting for me there is my own personal inner guide. My guide is any I choose to imagine. I enjoy being in this special place with this special friend.

My guide hands me a sacred computer disk. Upon it is all the secrets of automatic communication, all the wisdom of those who have gone before and all those to come. I receive it all. I take that disk to another room and give it to the automatic hiero-scripting librarian who places it in my deepest mind. This endowment for my art is funded by my higher consciousness.

✔ **I Ask For Information**

Just like automatic writing, I may hiero-script with no structured plan or I may ask for answers to specific questions; like- What is my life's purpose? How can I create more abundance? How can I improve the quality of my life?

I can ask for guidance from God, Spirit or a famous artist. I can request diagrams from the deceased; a loved one, a friend, a famous person, a past life. I can "regress" back into my childhood and clarify something I may have blocked or forgotten and then I can heal. Information from the past helps me understand and fulfill my life's purpose.

I can "progress" into the future; pinpointing a specific space in time or randomly into my future in this lifetime or another. Many artists use this technique to create and enhance their work.

Destinations For Hiero-scripting:

✍ Explore my deepest mind
✍ Achieve goals
✍ Answer my questions
✍ Channel guides
✍ Tap my unlimited creativity

Whatever I choose, I allow any information to emerge from my deepest wisdom without censor. I can decipher and make sense of it later.

✔ **I Create**
I take a deep, full breath, all that my lungs can comfortably hold, and I gently let it out. I do not judge, analyze or think. I'm not concerned if it makes sense- it might not at first. I draw, scribble or doodle anyway. I let all impulses move through my nervous system to the pen or brush onto the page. I Let my pen move on the paper as if it had a life of it's own and let whatever comes come. At first, I might scribble a doodle, draw lines and shapes or random words and impressions. I let them come. No matter what, I don't stop. I continue to move words or record my random thoughts. Eventually, I find messages – lots of them.

AUTO SUGGESTIONS FOR HIERO-SCRIPTING

Another way to hiero-script is to record in my own voice the following set of instructions accompanied by soft recorded music.

"I bless myself on all levels making sure that all of these teachings are for my highest good. I put my feet on the floor. Take a deep breath through my body- (pause) Let it out. One more breath to the brain. Let it go. I Close my eyes.

For just a second, I imagine I have just been programmed with a disc that allows me to flow images on paper. I simply let these images move through my right or left hand. I flow with the pen, paints or media that I choose. I don't think, analyze, editor judge: just simply let the images put themselves across my paper or easel. I'm not concerned if it makes sense, it probably won't at first. I won't worry about; I just do it!

I take another deep breath. Let it out. Put my pen or brush upon the paper as I let it flow. I take another full breath. Good."

SPECIAL DESTINATIONS FOR HIERO-SCRIPTING

Hiero-Scripting lets me travel my inner wisdom as:

✍ **I Explore My Deepest Mind**
Mandalas Self Portraits Self Therapy Family Portraits People as Patterns People as Colors, Draw a house

✍ **I Achieve Goals**
Healing Portraits Charting My Life

✍ **I Answer Questions**
Doorways of Truth Indian Dream Scapes

✍ **I Channel My Guides**
Spirit Guide Portraits, Dial Van Gogh

✍ **I Tap My Unlimited Creativity**
Creativity Circles

I EXPLORE MY DEEPEST MIND

Mandalas - Draw a house - Self Therapy - Self Portraits -
Family Portraits - People as Patterns - People as Colors -

MANDALAS

✍ Draw A Circle
✍ I Get Centered
✍ I Draw

Mandalas, or drawing within the confines of a circle, are an exciting way to capture my symbolic wisdom on paper. When I'm done drawing, I might want to write words to describe what the drawing means to me. Or tell someone about my drawing. Or put my mandalas on the wall, one next to the other. Over time, their beauty takes on new understanding and meaning for me. I will particularly enjoy looking at them in sequential order.

✔ **Draw a Large Circle**
I get a large piece of paper and draw a circle about the size of a 78 record. (Remember those?) I make sure to have marking pens, crayons, or colored pencils available.

✔ **I Get Centered**
If I want I can take 3 cleansing breaths , use self hypnosis or get centered any way that I know works best for me. Playing soothing music is very helpful as well.

Bless me on all levels
Physically, mentally, emotionally and spiritually
So I may truly recognize and fulfill my life's purpose
and let all teachings be for the highest good of myself and
humanity.
Help me reconnect with my special gifts and let me lovingly shed
any negative messages given by insensitive people.
Thank you. Amen. Awomen.

✔ I Let My fingers Do The Drawing

I let the colors create the image. It is important that, while I draw, do not think or analyze. I think of this as not an exercise in art,but an exercise of energy release.

Mandala
by Shelley

Draw a House - by Larissa (age 4)

DRAW A HOUSE

✎ I Get Centered

✎ Draw A House To My Specifications

When I draw a house I am actually symbolically presenting myself as I experience life. When I analyze my drawing, it's a good idea to notice how I fortify the walls. Are there people in my drawing? Are there trees and plant life outside? This usually represents how much I like people or vitality around me. It's fascinating to do this exercise often and notice how it changes or shifts.

SELF THERAPY

- ✍ I Get Centered
- ✍ I Bless Myself
- ✍ I Ask For Clarification
  Of Limiting Attitudes

SELF PORTRAITS

- ✍ I Get Centered
- ✍ I Bless Myself
- ✍ I Draw A Picture Of Myself:
  As a Child
  Now, In The Future

Self Portrait - by Larissa (age 4)

FAMILY PORTRAITS

- ✍ I Get Centered
- ✍ Bless Myself
- ✍ I Draw 3 Pictures:
  1. Of The Family Of My Childhood
  2. My Family Now
  3. My Family in the Future

Poem 1

Mother loves me forever.
Father is there 'til the end
Brothers and sisters, best
I'm never in need of a frei

Truth is the mode of communing.
Laughter: the tone of the day.
My talents and reams are encouraged.
"You're terrific" is what they all say.

My energy bubble elation.
I relax right up too the soul.
Love and peace are so easy.
I am healthy, happy, and whole.

Poem 2

Mother abondoned me early.
Daddy beat me instead.
My sister and brother betray me.
I was sexually molested in bed.

Family secrets are sacred.
Survival: the tone of the day.
My talents and dreams are insulted.
"You're a loser" is what they all say.

My energy's always hysteric.
To stop the pain is my goal.
Shame, guilt, rage, and heartache
Keep me sad and out of control.

Family Portraits

PEOPLE AS PATTERNS

In this process I Hiero-script symbols that resonate for myself and others. I can use these symbols as a focal point for meditation. Often the symbols that emerge are hieroglyphics from the indigenous ones, ancient sacred geometry, Sanskrit,, Hindu, Tantric, Ayurvedic and Hebraic letters. One lovely lady from Kansas City, Penny, draws ancient tribal symbols which when pieced together formed a larger picture: puzzle pieces with mysterious meanings. Imagine her surprise when she found a chart for the structure of DNA that matched her puzzle!

- ✍ Music
- ✍ Blessing
- ✍ I Get Centered
- ✍ I Tune In
- ✍ I Draw/ Write/ Image/ Color What I Receive

✔ **Music**
If desired

✔ **Blessing**
Bless me on all levels
Physically, mentally, emotionally and spiritually
So I may truly recognize and fulfill my life's purpose
and let all teachings be for the highest good of myself and humanity.
Help me reconnect with my special gifts and let me lovingly shed any negative messages given by insensitive people.
Thank you.Amen. Awomen

✔ **I Get Centered**
"I take a deep breath"

Release and relax and get into center I invite Mr../ms editor to step aside until I complete this exercise. He/she can help later if I need them to refine my drawings

✔ **Tune In**

"I easily receive symbols that resonate with this being"

I now tune in or focus my energy toward another. If they are present, I place my hand on their forehead. If they aren't present I think about them and imagine my hand on their forehead. I let their energy translate into my hands as symbol, shape, pattern or color. When I get a sense that I am ready, I...

✔ **I Draw/ Write/ Image/ Color What I Receive**

People as Patterns
by Shelley

PEOPLE AS COLORS PROCESS

In this process I resonate myself and others as colors.

- ✍ **Abundance of Paper Canvas and Colors**
- ✍ **Music**
- ✍ **Blessing**
- ✍ **I Get Centered**
- ✍ **I Tune In**
- ✍ **I Let The Color Spill Upon My Page**

People as Colors Process
by Shelley

I ACHIEVE GOALS

Healing Portraits
Charting My Life

HEALING PORTRAITS

- ✐ A Nice Blank Page
- ✐ I Get Centered
- ✐ Draw A Portrait Of Myself Or My Family As I'd <u>Like</u> It To Be... Perfect In Every Way.

CHARTING MY LIFE

- ✐ A Nice Blank Page
- ✐ I Get Centered
- ✐ I Map My Life From Beginning To End
- ✐ I Map My Life From This Moment Forward As I'd <u>Like</u> It To Be... Perfect In Every Way.

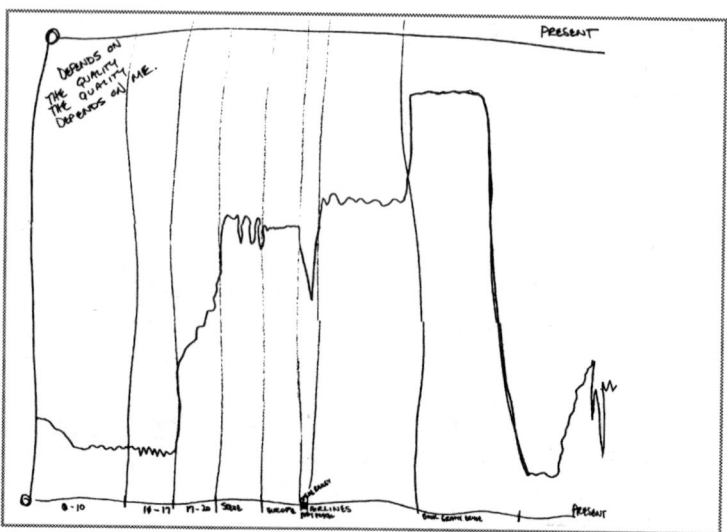

Life Graph

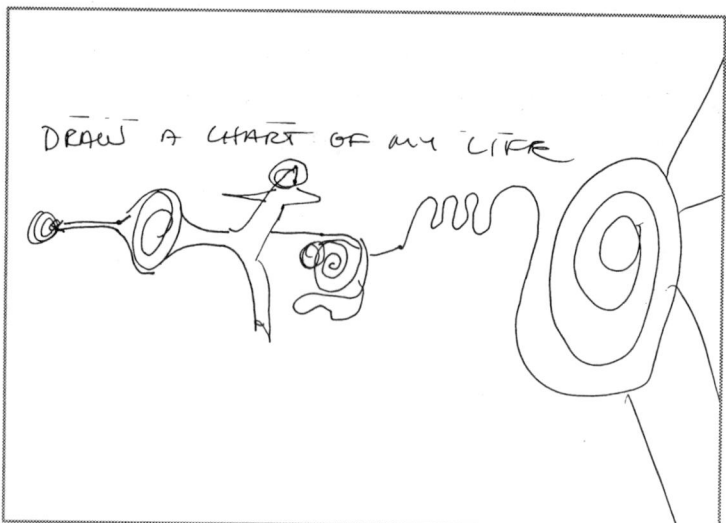

Life Chart

I ANSWER QUESTIONS

Doorways of Truth
Indian Dream Scapes

DOORWAYS OF TRUTH

This is a fabulous way for me to receive answers to my most gripping questions. It's sometimes a good idea to ask the same question several days in a row and look at all the "answers" at the same time

- ✍ I Ask A question
- ✍ Draw A Door
- ✍ Open The Door
- ✍ I Draw What I Find On The Other Side
- ✍ I Write My Question On The Top Of The Page
- ✍ Divert My Attention and Get My Answer

✔ **I Ask A Question**
I think of a question that I would like answered then I let the question go. I gently blow it off and away.

✔ **I Draw A Door**
I draw a picture of a door noting its textures and colors. The door has a sign on it I draw the sign.

✔ **I Open The Door**
In my mind's eye I open the door noticing how easily or gently it opens.

✔ **I Draw What I Find On The Other Side**
I draw what ever pops upon my page as I imagine what I find on the other side of my door. When I am done I...

✔ **Write My Question On The Top Of The Page**

✔ I Divert My Attention and Get My Answer

I take my attention elsewhere. I go get a glass of water or take a stroll. I'm now ready to return with "fresh eyes" and I observe how my drawing answers my question.

INDIAN DREAM SCAPES

Some societies (Sonoi, Aborigine and many others) believe that the dream state is reality and the waking state is an illusion. Indiginous ones like the Indians go on vision quests to seek a dream for their path and pupose. I can do the same with hieroscripting.

✎ I Imagine Myself In Nature

✎ I Get Centered and Bless Myself,
  (I may burn sage or incense if I like)

✎ I Ask To Enter The Dream World

✎ I Draw

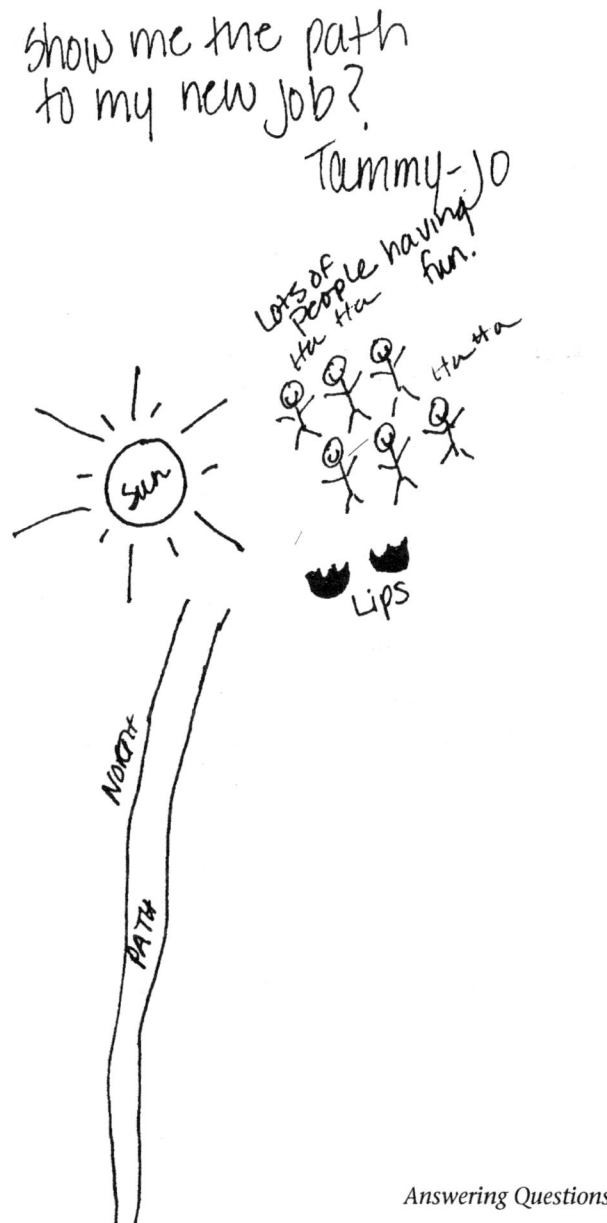

Answering Questions

I CONTACT MY SPIRIT GUIDES

Spirit Guide Portraits
Dial Van Gogh

SPIRIT GUIDE PORTRAITS

- ✍ A Nice Blank Page
- ✍ I Get Centered With My Prayer Of Protection
- ✍ I Ask For A Specific Guide

  Or request any Loving Angel, ET, Ascended Master, or Deceased Loved One To Present Themselves Upon My Page Or Canvas

- ✍ I Imagine That They Draw Or Paint Themselves Through My Hand
- ✍ I Thank Them And Clear Myself When I'm Done

DIAL VAN GOGH

- ✍ A Nice Blank Page

- ✍ I Get Centered With My Prayer Of Protection

- ✍ I Think Of An Artist I Would Like To Emulate
  ie: VanGogh, Picasso, Michaelangelo

- ✍ I Notice Their Energy

- ✍ I Imagine That They Assist Me As Draw Or Paint

- ✍ I Thank Them And Clear Myself When I'm Done

Spiritual Guide Portrait
by Bibi

I TAP MY UNLIMITED CREATIVITY

Creativity Circles

CREATIVITY CIRCLES

✍ **A Nice Blank Page**

✍ **I Draw 25 to 50 Circles On Each Page.**
Each About The Size Of A Silver Dollar

✍ **I Get Centered**

✍ **I Turn Each Circle Into An Item It Reminds Me Of**

Creativity Circles

Self Portrait By Shelley

Shelley Lessin Stockwell

Internationally respected speaker, educator, Transpersonal Hypno-therapist, and psychic channel, Shelley Lessin Stockwell delivers lectures, key note addresses and seminars that get results. Her customized, experiential presentations are gleaned from 25 years of experience.

Shelley teaches no-nonsense methods and simple-to-use exercises to create financial, physical, social and emotional well-being. She turns self-defeating attitudes into uplifting patterns, turmoil into positive energy, and work into fun.

Ms. Stockwell is a newspaper columnist and the author of five books, fifteen cassettes and two videos. A regular guest on TV and radio talk shows. She was recently featured on NBC's "The Other Side", "The Phil Donahue Show" and the "Channel 9 News".

Her popular television program "The Shelley Show" won an Angel Award of Excellence for outstanding cable television. Her book: *Sex and Other Touchy Subjects* was given the Gift of the Year Award by the International Family Health Council of the Pacific.

Her books include:

Insides Out

Sex and Other Touchy Subjects

Time Travel: Do-It-Yourself Past Life Journey Handbook

Automatic Writing and Hiero-scripting:
Tap Unlimited Creativity and Guidance

Denial Is Not A River In Egypt:
Unveil Denial, Depression and Addiction and Feel Terrific

Shelley has just returned from her 3rd trip to Egypt where she spoke at the Great Pyramid of Giza. Her newest cassette tape; *Mer Ka Ba: Ascension to the Fourth Dimension* lets the listener experience a sacred ancient Egyptian initiation rite of passage.

TRANCE-FORMATIONS

HYPNOSIS, CHANNELING & PAST LIFE REGRESSIONS
(VIDEO TAPE)

by
Shelley Lessin Stockwell

This video will transform the way you see yourself once and for your highest good!

Shelley Lessin Stockwell's Trance-Formations is a riveting opportunity to explore the deepest regions of your mind through hypnosis, channeling and past life regression.

Demonstrates:

- ★ Channeling
- ★ Hypnosis
- ★ Regressions
- ★ Progressions
- ★ Automatic Writing
- ★ Behavior Modification

Available in Japanese too!

$19.95
Video Tape
ISBN #0-912559-23-3

SELF-HYPNOSIS AUDIO CASSETTES

Closed eye meditations by **Shelley Lessin Stockwell**

Only $10.00 each!

Automatic Writing
Journey - activate the sub-conscious and release your creative self!   ISBN #0-912559-21-7

Time Travel
Access past & future lives with this do-it-yourself hypnosis cassette.   ISBN #0-912559-21-7

No More Sugar Junkie
No more sugar blues, feel alive; terrific!
ISBN #0-912559-03-9

Mer-Ka-Ba: Ascension to the 4th Dimension
Powerful consciousness expansion for your highest good.
ISBN #0-912559-11-X

Yes, You Can Quit Smoking
Save money, breathe again and feel healthy.
ISBN #0-912559-04-7

Yes, I Can!
Achieve your personal goals & highest potentials. ISBN #0-912559-09-8

Sleep, Beautiful Sleep
Sleep soundly and feel rested, at home or away. Good stress reduction.   ISBN #0-912559-01-2

Peace and Calm
The perfect stress reducer. You need no tranquilizers.
ISBN #0-912559-08-X

Flight Attendant Well-Being
A perfect attitude adjuster. Face passengers feeling positive, happy.   ISBN #0-912559-05-5

Lose Weight!
Lose unwanted pounds forever, gaining energy and confidence.   ISBN #0-912559-02-0

No More Alcohol
Break free of alcohol. Feel your life again.
ISBN #0-912559-10-1

Shelley Stockwell's self-hypnosis cassettes teach you to shed antiquated negative habits and replace them with the good habits you want for yourself.

"Thank you Shelley for giving me - ME!"
–C.M., Grand Forks, ND

"Your tapes have been a real blessing in my life"
– D.R., San Francisco, CA

"FANTASTIC! You wonderful, crazy, creative woman. Thanks for sharing so much with everyone."
– V.R., Los Angeles, CA

$10.00 Each
Self-Hypnosis Audio Cassettes
60 Minutes Each

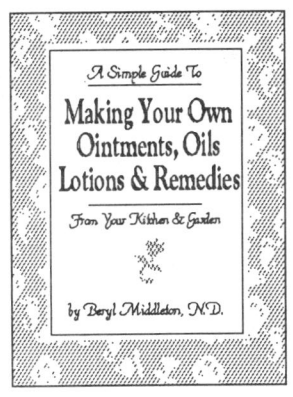

U R WHAT U EAT
& THE DINOSAUR RAP

Created By
Shelley Lessin Stockwell, Hypnotherapist
Kathy Felker, Registered Dietitian &
famous puppeteer
Betsy Moreland, Special Education Teacher
Frank Unzuata, "The Magic Music Man"
Spike, your basic dinosaur

"Teaches children an important nutritional message, while
providing catchy refrains. Reggae inspired embellishments
make pleasant listening for adults as well. Weightwatchers
could use this book for positive auto-suggestion"

– Focus on Books

"The perfect antidote to junk food"   – Judy Pastel, Mother, MFCC

$10.00
Audio Cassette - 22 Minutes
ISBN #0-912559-14-4

MOMMY BUNNY'S
GOING TO WORK

By **Shelley Lessin Stockwell**

"A simple, reassuring song & story that can help parents enor-
mously in dealing with their children's abandonment anxiety"
– Ellen Hokanson, Focus on Books

"Before MOMMY BUNNY, Ryan threw a fit when I went to work.
Now, he's happy and I don't feel guilty!"
– Gayle Tritz, Flight Attendant

"Mommy rabbit left. Baby rabbit is happy and says I love you
Mommy"   – Suzy Brown, Age 4

$10.00
Audio Cassette
ISBN #0-912559-16-0
ISBN #0-912559-06-3
(Flight Attendant Version)

Now you can play
GREAT GOLF!

By **Shelley Lessin Stockwell**
and **Dr. John Goode**

**"Great Golf is a game played on a
6 inch course – the space between
your ears."**   – Bobby Jones

This powerful program of "Great Golf" gets results! You will:

- ✓ Improve
- ✓ Free your mind
- ✓ Build confidence
- ✓ Play focused & relaxed
- ✓ Feel your best

Daily mental and physical practice truly makes you a perfect
golfer. Your success with the Great Golf program is unlimited!

$10.00
Audio Cassette - 60 Minutes
ISBN #0-912559-20-9

MER•KA•BA:
ASCENSION TO THE
4TH DIMENSION

By **Shelley Lessin Stockwell**
Tonal Music by **Wayne Perry**

14 Breaths to Enlightenment!
Powerful consciousness
expansion for your highest
good! Learn the ancient
Egyptian initiation rite as you
expand your consciousness.

"A powerful and mind altering experience not to be missed!"
– Kay Risberg, Hypnotist

$10.00
Book
ISBN #0-912559-26-8

INSIDES OUT

by
**Shelley
Lessin
Stockwell**

Plain talk poetry
guaranteed to
speak to you
where you really
live. If you want
to awaken your
vitality and truly
enjoy yourself,
this is your book!

"...Sprinkled throughout are short thoughts and quippy asides
– amusing and anecdotal"   – Focus on Books

"A beautiful, heart touching book. I urge you all to read it."
                                                 – Toni Grant, KABC Talk Radio

"There is a lot of humor in this book, but you can learn a lot
too. There is wisdom along with the humor... it's really a
fantastic book."   – Madelyn Camrud, WDAZ ABC-TV

"Shows how poetry can help see inside yourself. Maybe you'll
like what you see."   – Bill Smith, Channel 11 News

$6.95
132 Pages / Perfect Bound
ISBN #0-912559-00-4
LCN #83-710-30

Give A Friend The Gift Of Love & Laughter!

Make someone happy! Send them a book or tape today!

Give us their name, address and any greeting you wish to send and we will mail it to them from you!

To order additional gifts for friends write on the back of this order form.

To: Name _____
your friend's name

Address _____

city _____ state ____ zip ____

My Salutation: _____

ORDERING INFORMATION
Please check the boxes of your choice (if more than one, please insert quantity)

★ **BOOKS**
- ☐ TIME TRAVEL - Past Life Handbook $19.95
- ☐ AUTOMATIC WRITING & HIEROSCRIPTING ....$ 7.50
- ☐ HYPNOSIS & CREATIVE WRITING ....$ 9.95
- ☐ SELF HYPNOSIS: SMILE/MONEY ....$ 9.95
- ☐ NUMEROLOGY: HOT NUMBERS.....................................$ 9.95
- ☐ SEX & OTHER TOUCHY SUBJECTS $14.95
- ☐ INSIDES OUT...$ 6.95
- ☐ DENIAL IS NOT A RIVER IN EGYPT $19.95
- ☐ BERYL'S HERBAL BLISS...$ 9.95

★ **SELF HYPNOSIS AUDIO CASSETTES**
- ☐ AUTOMATIC WRITING..$10
- ☐ TIME TRAVEL............$10
- ☐ MER-KA-BA.............$10
- ☐ YES! I CAN...............$10
- ☐ PEACE AND CALM...$10
- ☐ LOSE WEIGHT..........$10
- ☐ NO MORE ALCOHOL .$10
- ☐ NO MORE SUGAR JUNKIE...$10
- ☐ YES, I CAN QUIT SMOKING .$10
- ☐ SLEEP, BEAUTIFUL SLEEP.......$10
- ☐ THE MONEY TAPE...............$10
- ☐ FLIGHT ATTENDANT WELL-BEING .$10
- ☐ GREAT GOLF $14.95

★ **KIDS AUDIO CASSETTES**
- ☐ MOMMY BUNNY'S GOING TO WORK $10
- ☐ U R WHAT U EAT...$10

★ **MUSIC AND SONG AUDIO CASSETTES**
- ☐ DEEP INTO A CALMING OCEAN..$10
- ☐ SEX & OTHER TOUCHY SUBJECTS $10

★ **VIDEO**
- ☐ TRANCEFORMATIONS: Hypnosis, Channeling & Past Life ..$19.95
- ☐ STATIC GRIT ON MY CD: Music Video $19.95

SUBTOTAL

(California residents add 8.25% sales tax)
Foreign countries please add $3.50 to the price for each publication.

PLUS $2.50 POSTAGE AND HANDLING PER ITEM

TOTAL

Please complete this page and send check or money order to:

CREATIVITY UNLIMITED PRESS
30819 Casilina Drive
Rancho Palos Verdes, CA 90275

Name _____

Address _____

city _____ state ____ zip ____

Phone: (_____) _____

Give A Friend The Gift Of Love & Laughter!

Make someone happy! Send them a book or tape today!

Give us their name, address and any greeting you wish to send and we will mail it to them from you!

To order additional gifts for friends write on the back of this order form.

To: Name _____
your friend's name

Address _____

_____
city   state   zip

My Salutation: _____

ORDERING INFORMATION

Please check the boxes of your choice (if more than one, please insert quantity)

★ **BOOKS**
- ☐ TIME TRAVEL - Past Life Handbook $19.95
- ☐ AUTOMATIC WRITING & HIEROSCRIPTING ....$ 7.50
- ☐ HYPNOSIS & CREATIVE WRITING ....$ 9.95
- ☐ SELF HYPNOSIS: SMILE/MONEY ....$ 9.95
- ☐ NUMEROLOGY: HOT NUMBERS....................................$ 9.95
- ☐ SEX & OTHER TOUCHY SUBJECTS $14.95
- ☐ INSIDES OUT.. $ 6.95
- ☐ DENIAL IS NOT A RIVER IN EGYPT $19.95
- ☐ BERYL'S HERBAL BLISS...$ 9.95

★ **SELF HYPNOSIS AUDIO CASSETTES**
- ☐ AUTOMATIC WRITING ..$10
- ☐ TIME TRAVEL............$10
- ☐ MER-KA-BA..............$10
- ☐ YES! I CAN...............$10
- ☐ PEACE AND CALM...$10
- ☐ LOSE WEIGHT..........$10
- ☐ NO MORE ALCOHOL .$10
- ☐ NO MORE SUGAR JUNKIE...$10
- ☐ YES, I CAN QUIT SMOKING .$10
- ☐ SLEEP, BEAUTIFUL SLEEP.......$10
- ☐ THE MONEY TAPE...............$10
- ☐ FLIGHT ATTENDANT WELL-BEING .$10
- ☐ GREAT GOLF $14.95

★ **KIDS AUDIO CASSETTES**
- ☐ MOMMY BUNNY'S GOING TO WORK $10
- ☐ U R WHAT U EAT...$10

★ **MUSIC AND SONG AUDIO CASSETTES**
- ☐ DEEP INTO A CALMING OCEAN...$10
- ☐ SEX & OTHER TOUCHY SUBJECTS $10

★ **VIDEO**
- ☐ TRANCEFORMATIONS: Hypnosis, Channeling & Past Life ..$19.95
- ☐ STATIC GRIT ON MY CD: Music Video $19.95

SUBTOTAL

(California residents add 8.25% sales tax)
Foreign countries please add $3.50 to the price for each publication.

PLUS $2.50 POSTAGE AND HANDLING PER ITEM

TOTAL

Please complete this page and send check or money order to:

♡

CREATIVITY UNLIMITED PRESS
30819 Casilina Drive
Rancho Palos Verdes, CA 90275

Name _____

Address _____

_____
city   state   zip

Phone: (_____) _____

Give A Friend The Gift Of Love & Laughter!

Make someone happy! Send them a book or tape today!

Give us their name, address and any greeting you wish to send and we will mail it to them from you!

To order additional gifts for friends write on the back of this order form.

To: Name _____
your friend's name

Address _____

city   state   zip

My Salutation: _____

ORDERING INFORMATION

Please check the boxes of your choice (if more than one, please insert quantity)

★ **BOOKS**
- ☐ TIME TRAVEL - Past Life Handbook $19.95
- ☐ AUTOMATIC WRITING & HIEROSCRIPTING ....$ 7.50
- ☐ HYPNOSIS & CREATIVE WRITING ....$ 9.95
- ☐ SELF HYPNOSIS: SMILE/MONEY ....$ 9.95
- ☐ NUMEROLOGY: HOT NUMBERS...................................$ 9.95
- ☐ SEX & OTHER TOUCHY SUBJECTS $14.95
- ☐ INSIDES OUT...$ 6.95
- ☐ DENIAL IS NOT A RIVER IN EGYPT $19.95
- ☐ BERYL'S HERBAL BLISS...$ 9.95

★ **SELF HYPNOSIS AUDIO CASSETTES**
- ☐ AUTOMATIC WRITING ..$10
- ☐ TIME TRAVEL.............$10
- ☐ MER-KA-BA..............$10
- ☐ YES! I CAN...............$10
- ☐ PEACE AND CALM...$10
- ☐ LOSE WEIGHT..........$10
- ☐ NO MORE ALCOHOL.$10
- ☐ NO MORE SUGAR JUNKIE...$10
- ☐ YES, I CAN QUIT SMOKING .$10
- ☐ SLEEP, BEAUTIFUL SLEEP.......$10
- ☐ THE MONEY TAPE...............$10
- ☐ FLIGHT ATTENDANT WELL-BEING .$10
- ☐ GREAT GOLF $14.95

★ **KIDS AUDIO CASSETTES**
- ☐ MOMMY BUNNY'S GOING TO WORK $10
- ☐ U R WHAT U EAT $10

★ **MUSIC AND SONG AUDIO CASSETTES**
- ☐ DEEP INTO A CALMING OCEAN.................................$10
- ☐ SEX & OTHER TOUCHY SUBJECTS $10

★ **VIDEO**
- ☐ TRANCEFORMATIONS: Hypnosis, Channeling & Past Life ..$19.95
- ☐ STATIC GRIT ON MY CD: Music Video $19.95

SUBTOTAL

(California residents add 8.25% sales tax)
Foreign countries please add $3.50 to the price for each publication.

PLUS $2.50 POSTAGE AND HANDLING PER ITEM

TOTAL

Please complete this page and send check or money order to:

♡

CREATIVITY UNLIMITED PRESS
30819 Casilina Drive
Rancho Palos Verdes, CA 90275

Name _____

Address _____

city   state   zip

Phone: (_____) _____

Give A Friend The Gift Of Love & Laughter!

Make someone happy! Send them a book or tape today!

Give us their name, address and any greeting you wish to send and we will mail it to them from you!

To order additional gifts for friends write on the back of this order form.

To: Name _____
your friend's name

Address _____

city   state   zip

My Salutation: _____

_____

ORDERING INFORMATION

Please check the boxes of your choice (if more than one, please insert quantity)

★ **BOOKS**
- ☐ TIME TRAVEL - Past Life Handbook $19.95
- ☐ AUTOMATIC WRITING & HIEROSCRIPTING ....$ 7.50
- ☐ HYPNOSIS & CREATIVE WRITING ....$ 9.95
- ☐ SELF HYPNOSIS: SMILE/MONEY ....$ 9.95
- ☐ NUMEROLOGY: HOT NUMBERS ....$ 9.95
- ☐ SEX & OTHER TOUCHY SUBJECTS $14.95
- ☐ INSIDES OUT ....$ 6.95
- ☐ DENIAL IS NOT A RIVER IN EGYPT $19.95
- ☐ BERYL'S HERBAL BLISS ....$ 9.95

★ **SELF HYPNOSIS AUDIO CASSETTES**
- ☐ AUTOMATIC WRITING ..$10
- ☐ TIME TRAVEL............$10
- ☐ MER-KA-BA.............$10
- ☐ YES! I CAN.............$10
- ☐ PEACE AND CALM...$10
- ☐ LOSE WEIGHT.........$10
- ☐ NO MORE ALCOHOL.$10
- ☐ NO MORE SUGAR JUNKIE...$10
- ☐ YES, I CAN QUIT SMOKING .$10
- ☐ SLEEP, BEAUTIFUL SLEEP.......$10
- ☐ THE MONEY TAPE...............$10
- ☐ FLIGHT ATTENDANT WELL-BEING .$10
- ☐ GREAT GOLF $14.95

★ **KIDS AUDIO CASSETTES**
- ☐ MOMMY BUNNY'S GOING TO WORK $10
- ☐ U R WHAT U EAT $10

★ **MUSIC AND SONG AUDIO CASSETTES**
- ☐ DEEP INTO A CALMING OCEAN $10
- ☐ SEX & OTHER TOUCHY SUBJECTS $10

★ **VIDEO**
- ☐ TRANCEFORMATIONS: Hypnosis, Channeling & Past Life ..$19.95
- ☐ STATIC GRIT ON MY CD: Music Video $19.95

SUBTOTAL

(California residents add 8.25% sales tax)
Foreign countries please add $3.50 to the price for each publication.

PLUS $2.50 POSTAGE AND HANDLING PER ITEM

TOTAL

Please complete this page and send check or money order to:

♡

CREATIVITY UNLIMITED PRESS
30819 Casilina Drive
Rancho Palos Verdes, CA 90275

Name _____

Address _____

city   state   zip

Phone: (_____) _____

Give A Friend The Gift Of Love & Laughter!

Make someone happy! Send them a book or tape today!

Give us their name, address and any greeting you wish to send and we will mail it to them from you!

To order additional gifts for friends write on the back of this order form.

To: Name _____
your friend's name

Address _____

_____
city   state   zip

My Salutation: _____

ORDERING INFORMATION
Please check the boxes of your choice (if more than one, please insert quantity)

★ **BOOKS**
- ☐ TIME TRAVEL - Past Life Handbook $19.95
- ☐ AUTOMATIC WRITING & HIEROSCRIPTING ....$ 7.50
- ☐ HYPNOSIS & CREATIVE WRITING ....$ 9.95
- ☐ SELF HYPNOSIS: SMILE/MONEY ....$ 9.95
- ☐ NUMEROLOGY: HOT NUMBERS.......................................$ 9.95
- ☐ SEX & OTHER TOUCHY SUBJECTS $14.95
- ☐ INSIDES OUT...$ 6.95
- ☐ DENIAL IS NOT A RIVER IN EGYPT $19.95
- ☐ BERYL'S HERBAL BLISS...$ 9.95

★ **SELF HYPNOSIS AUDIO CASSETTES**
- ☐ AUTOMATIC WRITING ..$10
- ☐ TIME TRAVEL.............$10
- ☐ MER-KA-BA..............$10
- ☐ YES! I CAN...............$10
- ☐ PEACE AND CALM...$10
- ☐ LOSE WEIGHT..........$10
- ☐ NO MORE ALCOHOL .$10
- ☐ NO MORE SUGAR JUNKIE...$10
- ☐ YES, I CAN QUIT SMOKING .$10
- ☐ SLEEP, BEAUTIFUL SLEEP.......$10
- ☐ THE MONEY TAPE...............$10
- ☐ FLIGHT ATTENDANT WELL-BEING .$10
- ☐ GREAT GOLF $14.95

★ **KIDS AUDIO CASSETTES**
- ☐ MOMMY BUNNY'S GOING TO WORK $10
- ☐ U R WHAT U EAT $10

★ **MUSIC AND SONG AUDIO CASSETTES**
- ☐ DEEP INTO A CALMING OCEAN...$10
- ☐ SEX & OTHER TOUCHY SUBJECTS $10

★ **VIDEO**
- ☐ TRANCEFORMATIONS: Hypnosis, Channeling & Past Life ..$19.95
- ☐ STATIC GRIT ON MY CB: Music Video $19.95

SUBTOTAL

(California residents add 8.25% sales tax)
Foreign countries please add $3.50 to the price for each publication.

PLUS $2.50 POSTAGE AND HANDLING PER ITEM

TOTAL

Please complete this page and send check or money order to:

♡

CREATIVITY UNLIMITED PRESS
30819 Casilina Drive
Rancho Palos Verdes, CA 90275

Name _____

Address _____

_____
city   state   zip

Phone: (_____) _____